THE POWER TO WRITE

THE
POWER
TO WRITE

A Writing Workshop in a Book

Caroline Joy Adams

CONARI PRESS

First published in 2003 by Conari Press,
an imprint of Red Wheel/Weiser, LLC
York Beach, ME

With offices at:
368 Congress Street
Boston, MA 02210
www.redwheelweiser.com

Cover Illustration and Interior Calligraphy: Caroline Joy Adams
Book Design: Maxine Ressler

Library of Congress Cataloging-in-Publication Data

Adams, Caroline Joy.
  The power to write : a writing workshop in a book / Caroline Joy Adams.
    p. cm.
Includes bibliographical references and index.
  ISBN 1-57324-809-6
  1. English language--Rhetoric. 2. Creative writing. 3. Title.
PE1408 .A27 2003
808'.02--dc21   2002153030

Printed in Canada
02 03 04 05 TCP 10 9 8 7 6 5 4 3 2 1

*Dedicated to my dearest daughter Christine,
a powerful young artist and writer who continues
to be my greatest inspiration . . .*

*and to Tony, whose bright, creative mind sparked my
own to new heights as I worked on this book . . .*

We are all WRITERS & READERS as well as communicators with the need at times to please & satisfy ourselves with the clear & almost perfect thought...

Roger Angell

Contents

A Note to Readers

The Power to Write is intended for *everyone* who wants to write but who may need a quick dose of inspiration to get going. For if you want to write—why not learn to write in a more *powerful* way? Powerful, inspired writing is writing that flows along easily, fueled by a sense of high energy. It's the kind of writing that makes the reader want to keep reading, because the story, long or short, based on real life or drawn purely from your imagination, is filled with feeling, an intriguing story line, and characters your readers come to care about.

Despite some myths to the contrary, too, writing is definitely an art that can be learned. For we are no more born writing than we are playing the piano, running a marathon, cooking a gourmet meal, or riding a bicycle. So of course we can all learn to write more powerfully than we may have imagined—and so can you. This book is here to serve as your own personal "Writing Workshop in a Book." It's designed to show you exactly *how* to infuse your writing with greater power and get you inspired enough to keep going once you've begun. And it will work equally well, whether you prefer writing in the privacy of your own home, or whether you want the stimulation of being with others who share your interest in expressing yourself through the written word and have decided to gather together in a formal or informal writing group to encourage one another's creative impulses. But whichever way you go— I know you'll have fun as you get in touch with your own natural and inborn power to write, deep within you just waiting to be unleashed.

Acknowledgments

I thank my daughter, Christie, first of all, for her bountiful love, wisdom, maturity, and cooperation while this book was in process. I'm a lucky mom, and I know it. Thanks also to my mother, Lynne Knudsen, for her continual support, love, enthusiasm, and very helpful editorial suggestions; and great thanks, too, to my father, Arvid Knudsen, my original inspiration for becoming an artist and writer. Thanks also once again to my second Mom, Jeanne Henderson, for her unwavering support and belief in me. And, thanks, too, to my sister, Nancy Knudsen, my brother-in-law, Jack La Forte, my brother David Knudsen, and nephews Dan Vidal and Nicholas Knudsen Canby, for their encouragement and loving support this past year. I am truly blessed to call them all family.

Thanks also to Tony Kord, for his expert editorial help, and for designing the *www.ThePowertoWrite.com* website; and to Leslie Berriman, my wonderful editor, who encouraged me to write this book in the first place—and to all the other fine Conari staff members who helped bring this book into being, including Brenda Knight, Rosie Levy, Heather McArthur, Leah Russell, Maxine Ressler, and Pam Suwinsky.

I also give thanks to Barnes and Noble in Hadley, Massachusetts, for helping give me the perfect atmosphere for my ongoing writing workshops—especially to Andrea Gallerani, who helped them get started, and to Sarah Clark, who continues to facilitate the process. Thanks, too, to all the men and women who have attended on a regular basis, especially Millicent Jackson, Cathleen Robinson, Rebecca Fricke, Ellen Evert Hopman, Vikki Gilbert, Ananda Lennox, Brenda Lyons, Jack Tannenbaum, Joe Lastowski, and Larry. You have been a powerful inspiration to me, each one of you—and this book could never have been written without you.

Also, great thanks to the other special friends who've inspired me or supported me long the way—Denise Schwartz, Hila Kummins, Lori Broussard, Bonnie Druschel, Janet Parker, Ana Gorman, Nell Corry, Cindy Kartch, Susie Mantell—and J.C. Tibbo, for her wonderful healing energy and always powerfully helpful words of wisdom. A special thanks, too, to Diana and Jeff Krauth, owners of the wonderful Beyond Words Bookshop, for having been the first store to carry my published work, now ten years ago. And, a special thanks to all the stores that still carry my books and Inspirations, and all those who have written me letters, by regular mail or email, to tell me how much my words have meant to them. Thanks so much for sharing your love and your words with me. It means more to me than you will ever know.

Introduction

What if, starting right now, you could take those glimmers of ideas that are swirling around in your mind and begin transforming them into powerfully told, intriguing stories, based on compelling real-life experiences or drawn purely from your imagination? If that's what you're secretly (or perhaps not-so-secretly) wishing you could easily do, you are definitely in the right place.

The Power to Write will inspire you to get excited about writing and fired up to get your sketchy ideas into solid, finished form, and will offer you, through each of seven keys, a concrete, easy-to-remember way to call forth your own most inspired words from within—no matter what kind of writing interests you most.

It may be that much of the writing you've done so far has been highly personal, gracing the pages of stashes of private journals. Or perhaps your affinity is for fiction, and you've written some short stories or maybe even started a novel. Or it may be that you have an inclination to write poetry, or aspire to write magazine articles based on some of your own life experiences or on other topics that intrigue you.

Then again, maybe you're not sure what you want to write, yet you know the urge to write *something* has overtaken you. If so, that's fine, too. All you need is a desire to get started, or to take your writing to the next level; for the essential keys to powerful writing apply no matter where you are on the writing pathway, or what kind of writing you may wish to try next.

The urge to write comes to most of us because we have a need to express ourselves in words, and we have ideas, insights, or story concepts we'd like to share. Yet whether you've been writing for years or are just beginning, I bet you'd like your writing to possess a certain power and polish that may seem hard to come by at times. I wouldn't be surprised, too, if you share the secret fear that most of us have: that we can't write anything truly worthwhile. This fear can stop us before we even set pen to paper, or prevent us from ever showing our writing to anyone else once it's finished.

If that same secret fear lurks deep within you, please know that this book is here to help. My goal is to help you work through that fear, and get your pen moving (even if the fear never goes away altogether). For I believe that the most important step toward dispelling your fear of not being a "good enough" writer is to learn some key concepts that can strengthen your writing skills. When you start to practice the new concepts you'll learn here, your skills will almost certainly take a giant leap forward. You'll then start to produce writing that's more alive, smooth flowing, and enticing to read—and that's when you'll find your fears will ease up and be replaced, bit by bit, by a newfound sense of confidence, exhilaration, and *inspiration*.

WHEN you
are able to write in
a more powerful &
elegant way, you'll find
it more fun
to write ...

Caroline Joy Adams

You have the
POWER
to Write...

So take up your pen, open your heart, your mind & your soul, & just let the words start flowing...

Caroline Joy Adams

Please note, too, that the "inspiration" to write is not a magical muse that falls down from the sky, blessing a lucky few who can then effortlessly pour out reams of perfect prose. Far from it. In reality, those writers who feel most inspired are almost always the ones who have taken the time to learn exactly *how* to create writing that has a more polished feel. When you, too, are able to write in a more powerful and elegant way, you'll simply find it more *fun* to write. And that enhanced sense of satisfaction and fun will very likely ignite your creative fires— and fan the flames of your inspiration to keep going.

Your goals, too, may include being published or speaking to a wide audience—or perhaps you simply want to write for yourself, your family, and your friends. Whichever the case may be, know that you are in a perfect starting place, right now. For no matter what, we're all just students: of life, of love, and of writing. We just may be at different levels, at different times. Yet we can all learn so much from one another, and the learning journey can be a wonderful adventure, with many unexpected and delightful surprises along the way.

We're about to undertake an exciting journey into the vast world of words together—one that's akin to taking a fun, fast-paced writing workshop, but best of all, one you can start any time, and take anywhere. I'm happy and deeply honored that you're joining me—so let's begin, right now, without delay.

Caroline Joy Adams
WILLIAMSBURG, MASSACHUSETTS
MAY 2002

Part I

Shape Your Words into an Intriguing Story

Know That You Have the Power to Write: Your Vast Memory Bank of Experiences and Feelings Can Help You Get Started

Key 1

JUST WHAT IS IT that drives *you* to the page, compels you to sit down and write, or makes you want to write, even if it's sometimes hard to get started? Do you feel the strongest need to get words out on paper when you are trying to sort out your emotions and daily life experiences? If so, have you filled thousands upon thousands of pages of private journals with such writings? But do you also sometimes wonder if you might be able to turn some of these musings into stories that could hold interest for others?

I want
to write
but more than that I
want to bring out all kinds
of things that lie buried
deep in my heart...
Anne Frank

Or does the urge to write come over you when the idea for a fictional story has captured your imagination, and dynamic or dreamlike scenes, replete with interesting characters and their life crises and challenges, float through your mind by day and night, just calling out to you to be set to life on paper? If so, is it your greatest fantasy or hope that your story might someday be worth publishing, so that others can enter the world of words you've created?

Whether our urge to write stems from a desire to recount true-to-life stories (nonfiction) or to spin tales that we make up altogether (fiction), I believe that we can all develop our innate capacity to tell compelling stories. At the same time, we can benefit from some guidance in just how to come up with a written story that feels complete, intriguing, and worthy of asking others to take the time to read. And such guidance in exactly how to translate your story ideas into completed form is what *The Power to Write: A Writing Workshop in a Book* is here to offer you.

What a Story Is

But just what is a story, anyway? Quite simply, short or long, one page or one thousand pages, a story is an interesting tale about something dramatic, funny, memorable, or intriguing that has happened to ourselves or to other real-life or fictional characters. It always contains at least one character who is faced with a challenge or conflict—major or minor—that he or she must try to resolve on some level by the story's end.

Your purpose in telling a story, as the writer, is to take your reader on a brief but potentially powerful emotional journey—as you entertain, inspire, or invite them, for a brief bit of time, to enter into the inner world of another human soul.

A good story also allows your reader to temporarily step beyond his or her own boundaries. More than anything, it invites the reader to feel what the character feels—and thus to feel less alone, more connected to others, and part of the larger circle of life for that short passage of time during which he or she is absorbed in your words. And that highly desirable, though not always easy-to-attain feeling of enhanced connection to other minds, lives, and souls is something we are all seeking to experience, almost all the time.

A story, no matter how short or long, too, nearly always revolves around a time of change in the life of the character—whether the character is you, describing your own life experience, or a fictional character you've created. Such a change may be huge or small, internal or external, one the character is choosing and initiating. Or, the change may be happening entirely against the character's will, one that he or she is valiantly struggling to prevent from taking place.

This impending change produces a sense of mounting tension—for if you have no tension (which is caused by the conflict at the center of the story), you have no story. For in life and in stories alike, it's tension and *trouble,* that truly intrigue people, and the hope that a resolution will occur that keeps them interested. Happy endings, of course, do happen and are fine in many cases. But entirely smooth-sailing lives, and stories, just don't hold our interest for long—for there's simply no staying or selling power in such strife-free tales.

Your goal, then, is to sweep your readers into your story, scene by scene, and pique their curiosity about the question that the conflict or tense situation raises, about what's going to happen next. And by story's end, you simply *must* answer that question, resolving the tension for your readers in a logical, at times surprising, but always satisfactory way.

But perhaps you are saying right now, What stories do *I* have to tell that others could possibly care about? Well, I can guarantee that no matter who you are—your age or life stage; your geographical location or occupation; your religious beliefs or political persuasion; your family background, marital status, or your current family makeup—you have potentially *hundreds* of stories to tell.

Possible Subjects

We all have potentially powerful stories deep within us, just waiting to be called forth, perhaps to be told aloud and then put into written words. Your storehouse of stories, too, flows from your many years of life *experience;* your unique *perspective* and way of seeing the world; and your ability to access a wide range of *feelings.* So let's consider just a few of the possibilities.

LOVE

Just like the rest of us, you've almost certainly had vast experience over the course of your lifetime with virtually everyone's number one interest: and that's *love*. And whether you know it now or not, you have a lot to say about this timeless topic. For love is the essence of life: and you've known many different kinds of love in your lifetime—from romantic forms of love to the love between parent and child, siblings, and friends. And if you've experienced deep struggles in any of these relationships (and haven't we all, at times?), you have a host of powerful memories to draw upon.

For instance: You've probably been in love, many more times than once—and then felt the agony of losing a love that you'd been certain would last forever. You've probably also felt the ache of being away from a lover for what felt like an eternity, only to ultimately experience a happy reunion. Or you may have felt the supreme sadness of loving someone who doesn't love you back, or who perhaps loves someone else—and you've been stung by the brutal nettles of betrayal. But whatever your unique experiences of love have been, there is no doubt that some of your most powerful and poignant moments could become the catalyst for deeply moving, potent stories—stories that nearly everyone can relate to.

WORK

Sigmund Freud once said that love and work are the two main human endeavors that we all pursue and have in common—and he may well have been right about that. You have almost certainly, then, had some powerful moments on your life pathway as you've traversed the world of work—regardless of what is happening for you now in that key aspect of life. Over time, you've probably held a host of different jobs—some of which you've loved, some of which you've hated, some of which you've perhaps been fired from unfairly—but all of which offer potentially interesting settings, characters, and dramatic moments that can trigger ideas for your stories.

PHYSICAL TRAUMA

Perhaps you've also, at one time or another, had a debilitating health condition, been in an accident, or known close friends or family members who've experienced such life dramas. Such situations can easily become the basis for a powerful piece of writing.

LOCATIONS

You've almost certainly lived in (or visited) a number of different houses, cities, and other geographical locations—some exotic, some perhaps seemingly plain as can be. You've also probably traveled a bit and had some unforgettable experiences on such journeys. But even a most ordinary setting or everyday trip in a car or bus can become the scene for an intriguing slice-of-life story.

PEOPLE

You've almost certainly (even if you've lived in the same town your entire life) known a host of different people, from teachers, to storekeepers, to ministers or rabbis or priests, aunts, uncles, neighbors, and others, whose lives have affected you and whose unique traits or life experiences can enter into the

Your personal memory bank of FEELINGS & EXPERIENCES *is your greatest resource as a writer...*

Caroline Joy Adams

drama of your stories. This applies equally whether you choose to focus on writing solely about true experiences, or to selectively take characteristics from real-life people and spin them into fictional characters.

FEELINGS

But more important, still, than your specific life experiences, is that you've undoubtedly *felt*, at one time or another, every human emotion possible—from wild joy to deep sadness and disappointment to outright fury. For virtually without exception, it's the underlying feelings that truly make for a powerfully told story: the feelings that your characters are experiencing, which you can bring forth and cause your *reader* to feel as he or she follows your story along.

So whether you choose to become a writer of fact or fiction, or to continually weave a fascinating fusion of the two, the most powerful way to get started writing is to tap directly into your huge memory bank of both life *experiences* and *feelings*. That's where you'll find an endless treasure trove of ideas to take off with and expand into story form—and from which truly inspired writing nearly always springs.

THE IMPORTANCE OF SHARING OUR STORIES

Sharing the stories of some of our most memorable moments of life can be a great gift. For at our very core, we have a *need* to share our stories—those about what has happened to us, and those that come to us through the marvelous realms of our imagination and end up as what we call fiction.

We need to tell our own stories and to listen to the stories of others, for these stories can serve many purposes. They can help others laugh at themselves, or at life, in moments when they most need to see the humor in otherwise difficult situations. At other times, our stories may help inspire someone to move beyond his or her own challenges—knowing that if you've been through something similar and survived, then perhaps he or she can, too.

Our stories matter. All of them. *Your* stories matter. So I urge you, right now, to go ahead, let your ideas flow, and start to get your stories out on paper—for you just never know how much of a difference they may make, and to whom.

FOCUS ON MEMORABLE LIFE MOMENTS

Here's what we'll be doing to start: I'll offer you topics that can get your memories fired up; you'll reflect a bit, then come up with an interesting moment or time in your life that relates to the topic suggested. You'll then put pen to paper, and take off with whatever comes, by writing a few paragraphs or pages. But first, let's take a look at some examples of the type of piece I'd like you to come up with.

The following story describes a moment in time when the narrator was overwhelmed by fear.

Black Ice

Suddenly there I was careening across the road, totally out of control, helplessly watching a maze of cars, like huge

Our stories matter...
Your stories matter...
for you just never
know how much of a
difference they make,
& to whom...

Caroline Joy Adams

lightning strikes, skating toward me across the black ice, coming at me from all directions; and I knew with certainty that my frantic, desperate attempts to press harder and harder on the brake pedal were futile, and I would *never* be able to stop on time.

I glanced at my three-year-old daughter sitting beside me, took in her small precious face, her innocent, enormous blue eyes turning toward me for comfort, but instead, I let out a wild, primal scream. Engulfed by my tidal wave of fear, a horrific high-pitched wail of her own then poured from her gut as her face crumpled in terror. I was sure, right then, that in a moment it would all be over and I'd never be able to hold her in my arms again and tell her how much I loved her.

Clearly the feared fatal accident didn't happen, as I'm here to tell the tale. This brief story-starter, though, portrays a moment when my life *could* have changed in a flash, and that's why it's stayed with me as a still-potent and emotionally charged memory. I was reminded of it because it happens to be winter right now, and silken waves of silvery snowflakes are fast falling down from the sky, whitening the narrow streets of my small New England town. Yet serene as the soft-looking snow appears, I am ever aware that underneath it lurks a sheet of potentially hazardous ice.

I offer this example because I want to emphasize to you that even if you haven't had many major life crises or dramas, I guarantee that you have lots of dramatic, interesting *moments* that can become the basis for a powerful piece of writing. And we can *all* transform our ordinary moments and daily experiences into stories that can become intriguing to others.

Let's move on to another example: A memorable evening, one that changed the course of my own life.

Across the Room

I had almost stayed home that fateful night, wanting nothing more than to settle down with a comforting cup of hot chamomile tea and a good book. But it was Friday night, once more, a lonely weekend approaching, and I knew, deep down, that after a year alone, it was high time I began to get out more and at least begin to open to the possibility of meeting someone new. So, shivering from the cold New England autumn air, even though I was wrapped up tight in my long black wool coat, my red skirt flying upward as the wind sent it soaring every few blocks, I walked the whole two miles downtown to the Cambridge "Y," to attend an English country dance for the very first time.

Before long I arrived, and soon after entering the large room, where the dance was already in progress, began to warm up. I noted, too, that the music was quite pleasant and soothing, and indeed there were a host of attractive men of various ages present, just as I'd been secretly hoping. So I joined in as best as I could.

But before long, I was feeling infinitely awkward, clumsy, my face flushed with embarrassment at my ineptness in catching on to the intricate steps that everyone else seemed to have done flawlessly all their lives. Confused as to which way my feet were supposed to move, fearing that I was simply *never* destined to be a dancer of any sort, I was starting to fantasize about just escaping quietly, slinking away from this sea of swiftly moving feet, arms, and legs, and flurries of faces, and back home to my lonely but familiar and comfortable little apartment.

Yet despite these persistent thoughts of leaving, I found myself still there, an hour later, whirling around the dance floor, getting dizzier by the minute—when suddenly I caught a glance of *him*, across the room. A new arrival, having come in late, he stood hesitantly, watching the crowd gracefully move across the floor to the rhythm of the live violin trio that was filling the air with a rather enchanting Bach piece. He seemed to be deciding whether to stay and join in, or to simply go on his merry way, to who knows where. In that very instant, mysteriously, but with an intensity far beyond anything I could explain—a stab of panic struck at my heart. Because I knew, already, that I wanted, *needed*, more than anything, for him to choose to stay. For I somehow sensed, with every fiber of my soul, that my entire destiny depended upon this split-second decision he was about to make.

I kept dancing, yet studying him intently at the same time, my eyes never leaving him, as he stood there. He seemed to be about twenty-three, a student-type, with clear, bright, but wistful-looking deep blue eyes that traveled intently around the room as if he, too, was looking for a lost someone—and was hoping, against hope, to find her here. Though he had an air of uncertainty about him, a sheepish, little-boy quality, he was undeniably handsome. He was exactly what I'd always thought of as my "type," with soft, brownish-blond hair, and a slight mustache, a medium build, and not too tall and not too short, about 5' 7" to my 5' 4". Just right.

A worn green backpack with a broken zipper, clearly filled with a stash of books, was slung upon his shoulder. Books, I imagined, to be filled with deep insights on philosophy, literature, and Renaissance art—as well as, of course, of volumes of romantic nineteenth-century poetry that I was already fantasizing he would soon be reading to *me*, late at night—in his place or mine, before turning out the lights, as we then reached out for the exquisite comfort of each other's warmth in the darkness.

For in some bizarre, surreal way, my future was flashing before me, and I *knew*—without yet knowing his name or his history, and not a one of his likes, dislikes, dreams, fears, or hopes—that he was the one I'd been searching for all my life, the man I was going to marry. And six months later, in one of the largest, most impressive churches in the great city of Boston, on the second day of May, as the clock struck twelve noon, surrounded by all those who knew and loved me—to my utter amazement—marry him I did.

This piece tells the story of the night I met my former husband—a meeting, now some fifteen years ago, that surely did change the course of my life. And "Across the Room" isn't a finished piece in itself, but like "Black Ice" is what I call a "story-starter"—a short vignette that *could* lead into a much more involved story. And the longer story *could* focus on any of the following topics: the early years of what at first seemed like a fairy-tale marriage; the ensuing very challenging seven years as the relationship unraveled; the divorce I endured when he left me; or the years of single parenting that I have traversed in the eight years since—all of which have given me numerous dramatic moments, episodes, and life insights to reflect on and write about.

But as is, this brief story-starter works to arouse interest in what happens next, for stories of how lovers met are almost always intriguing. What helps here, also, are the many details that give a sense of the setting, the scene, and the young characters involved.

Now It's Time for You to Get Started Writing

Now I invite *you* to get started writing, and as you proceed throughout this book with each of the Writing Practices, please keep the following three points in mind.

I. CONSIDER THIS A SEVEN-WEEK COURSE IN MORE POWERFUL WRITING

You may, if you like, consider the seven chapters that make up this book to be a seven-week course in the art of writing more powerful, compelling, and complete true-to-life or fictional stories. If you choose to use the book in this way, you may want to take time once or twice a week to read through the material on each key, and then work on each of the Writing Practices; and within a seven-week period you will undoubtedly experience a dramatic improvement in your writing.

It may help to consider each key, and the suggested Writing Practices for each, as a weekly assignment. However, please feel free to proceed in *any* time frame, or in any way that works best for you—just take it at whatever pace feels right. Take as much time for each Writing Practice as you wish—though you may want to allot one half-hour to one full hour at a time at first.

2. WRITE ABOUT TOPICS THAT TRULY CAPTIVATE YOU

If one topic among those suggested within each Writing Practice doesn't spark your creative flame, then find another that does. Or write about anything else that comes to mind. The topic is nowhere near as important as your commitment to sitting down, getting pen to paper, or opening a brand new file on your computer, and getting the words to start flowing.

3. WRITE BY HAND OR ON A COMPUTER

Whichever way works best for you is fine, though if you are used to doing most of your writing on a computer, it can be enormously useful to try writing by hand at times. So if you don't already do so, get some lined notebooks and take them with you wherever you go. That way *whenever* an interesting idea or thought or string of words comes to you, you'll be ready to capture it before it slips away from memory.

For you never know: You may find yourself one afternoon sitting in a café, sipping a cappuccino, breathing in the strong, rich, aromatic scent of coffee that's wafting through the air—when the urge to write overcomes you, and you can pull out your handy notebook. And you'll be glad you remembered to bring it with you. (It may make you feel more like a "real" writer—when others see you scribbling away, mysteriously, in your notebook, as they flip through the daily paper.) Maybe someone at the next table will even glance at you wistfully, strike up a conversation, and ask if you are a writer—and if so, just say, "Yes!" without hesitation. It'll be great for your self-confidence, and perhaps be the needed boost your ever-sensitive ego is craving—and it might just make you *feel* inspired to keep those words a-flowing!

Also, if you like, go out and buy some new pens that have a smooth feel, the kind that make you really *want* to put them to use. Keep them close by, wherever you are—and do commit to writing by hand at least some of the time. If you give it a chance, I think you'll find it truly can be an enjoyable, enlightening, and mind-expanding experience.

WRITING PRACTICE #1

It's now time to put pen to paper. When you are ready, write anything from two paragraphs to two pages, or more. However many words flow out will be just fine, so just relax into the process as much as possible. If an imaginary scene comes to you rather than something you've experienced in real life, that's fine, too. Some people find fiction comes much more easily than real-life experience: if that turns out to be true for you, even if it takes you by surprise, just go with it.

First, I'd like you to think of a moment in time when you were experiencing a deep emotion, such as I described in "Black Ice." If it helps, you may wish to think of a time when you were experiencing a deep emotion because of a difficult *interaction* you were having with someone—such as a parent, child, spouse, or other significant person in your life.

Remember to describe what was happening, how you were *feeling,* and what you were thinking. You may choose the same emotion I used—fear—or whatever other emotion comes to mind, such as joy, excitement, hope, anger, or sadness. I have also listed some possible writing topics, which may be helpful in triggering moments of deep emotion from your own life. Choose to write about one of these if something comes to you—or focus on any other emotional moment you like.

POSSIBLE TOPICS

- ✧ Write about a time when something extraordinarily disturbing happened to you and you were desperate to tell someone, but felt that you couldn't.

- ✧ Write about a time when you felt terribly betrayed.

- ✧ Write about a time when another person was furious with you and you felt it was unjustified.

↜ Write about a moment of deep regret . . . or, a moment when you were absolutely *elated* because of something wonderful that had happened or you knew was about to happen.

↜ Write about a time when you experienced a powerful loss and how you coped during the first few days afterward.

↜ Write about a time you were fired from a job . . . or when you *started* a new job that you were extremely excited about.

↜ Write about a time when you were forced to move against your will . . . or when you moved to new place that you *loved* . . . or hated.

WRITING PRACTICE #2

Now I'd like you to write about a moment when you met someone for the first time who was to have a huge impact on your life—such as in the scene I described in "Across the Room." Use details to describe this person, such as where you were when you met and how the person appeared, and be sure to convey a sense of the *feelings* flowing through you in the moments you are choosing to share.

SUMMARY

Key #1: Know That You Have the Power to Write: Your Vast Memory Bank of Experiences and Feelings Can Help You Get Started

Now that you've done a bit of writing, how does it feel? I hope that you've allowed yourself to just get started, without worrying about perfection in your writing, of any sort, at this stage. Later we'll get to the editing process. For now, I just want you to have fun and get into the creative flow!

Keep these three basic truths in mind, too, and you'll make giant leaps forward in your writing in no time: (1) You *can* learn to write more powerfully; (2) Your personal memory bank can be a vast and rich resource for your writing; and (3) Powerful writing always focuses on a conflict that leads to a resolution.

Never forget, too, that *your* stories, *your* words, are important. Your writing has the power to affect another's life, perhaps in the deepest way possible. So don't hold back. Let your words pour forth, and allow us the chance to listen to all that you have to share.

Start Your Story with a Powerful Opening

Key 2

IF YOU COME AWAY with only one new idea from this book, let it be this: Open your story with an intriguing first sentence or paragraph that will captivate your readers' attention and interest *immediately*. Apply this key to your writing whether your story is one page or one thousand, full of facts or pure fiction: for it always helps to start your story from a place of strength. I believe it's rarely worth making an exception to this rule.

Writing is fueled
by your creative
life force...

which once unleashed has its
own mysterious power... just
as words themselves do...

Caroline Joy Adams

In journalism, a powerful opening is known as a "lead," which serves an extremely important purpose for your readers, but also for you, the writer. First of all, it sets the mood and tone for what's to come, conveys a sense of dynamic, living energy to your story, arouses interest and curiosity, and entices your readers to *keep* reading.

Equally important, starting with a powerful opening gives you the momentum to keep going, to get the words flowing out with ease once you've started writing. Why? I believe it's because writing is fueled by your creative life force—which once unleashed has its own mysterious power. And part of this power comes not just from the story concept but from the exact words that you choose to use as you open a story. For I believe that words *themselves* have great power—over your reader, and for you, the story creator.

Power and Energy Exist in Every Word

Just consider this for a moment: Each of the more than 100,000 words that are part of our general vocabulary was once created, by *someone,* some time ago—that is, by a real live, flesh-and-blood person who first uttered this word as a *symbol* to describe a certain person, place, thing, feeling, mood, or action that was important to him or her at the time. And those word-symbols, of course, were first spoken aloud before ever finding their way into *written* symbol form.

Right from the start, the sounds that were chosen for a given word had to embody the concept the person was trying to name with that word-sound-symbol. Each word, then—as it was created—was infused with an expressive *energy,* an intuitive feeling, which represented an image and called forth a concept of that word in the listener's mind.

Take, for instance, the word *thunder.* It surely possesses the *feeling* of a hard, drumming sound, reminiscent of the real experience of hearing thunder during a storm. On the other hand, the word *summer* has a sweetness and lightness to it, bringing up an immediate feeling of languishing, long, expansive days and nights. But a word like *kill* has a harsh, abrupt, ominous sound, true to its meaning. By way of contrast, a word like *light,* or *love,* has a soft, lilting, comforting sound-feeling.

Nearly all words, aside from their actual meanings, are naturally laden with a special inherent energy of their own. And this energy brings up an immediate feeling in us, whether we hear a word spoken aloud by someone else; whether we speak it to ourselves as we read; or whether we say the word silently to ourselves as we write it down. It's important, then, even as we begin a story, to consciously choose words that call forth rich, resonant, symbolic, colorful images to our minds while we are engaged in the act of writing. These potent words will then automatically engage *our* attention, infuse us with deep feeling, and raise our creative storytelling energy to a higher level.

WE HAVE ONLY THIRTY SECONDS TO GRAB OUR READERS' ATTENTION

In just a few moments, you'll be creating some powerful story openings of your own, which I hope will excite you to the point that you'll really want to go ahead and write the rest of your story. But first, let's go back to our potential readers for a moment, as we consider this undeniable truth: We who inhabit the fast-paced, information-overloaded world of the twenty-first century are busier than ever, and more easily distracted. We have less time and shorter attention spans than ever—perhaps in the whole history of humankind.

Nearly every day, too, with lightning speed, most of us scan the Internet, the television screen, and the daily newspaper (and also, at times, magazines or books on the local bookstore shelves), seeking something that grabs our immediate attention.

If a given article, story, editorial, essay, or book doesn't light our inner fire in a matter of about thirty seconds—that's it. We skip to something else we hope will enthrall us. But why just a scant *thirty seconds?* Here's the reason: A couple of typical opening paragraphs of an article, story, or book contain about one hundred, or perhaps at most, 150 words. And most of us read at the rate of 200–300 words per minute, or about five words per second—meaning that in one-half a minute, we'll take in precisely that first hundred or so words on a page.

Almost everyone, too, makes that split-second decision to keep reading a given piece—or to stop dead in their tracks—after scanning those first hundred words. So we really have just a one-hundred-word, thirty-second window of opportunity to engage our readers' attention. We've simply *got* to light the fire of burning curiosity in our readers to hear the rest of what we've got to say in that brief half-moment of time—because we're not likely to be granted a second chance.

Do whatever it takes, then, to make those first hundred words of your story irresistibly intriguing, funny, dramatic, or beautifully descriptive—and you will vastly increase your chances of pulling your readers into your story line and keeping them there for the duration.

Remember that your story doesn't need to contain a life-or-death drama to be captivating, either. You may be writing a piece that's meant to be hilarious rather than heartbreaking, or a nonfiction personal-experience story or article that centers around handling a young child's temper tantrum rather than a terrible, traumatic life crisis.

But whatever your subject matter, story length, or ultimate purpose, you *can* get your story off to a roaring start through a powerful opening. So in those elegantly put-together, well-crafted, very first few sentences, aim to achieve this goal: Encapsulate the *most* intriguing essence of the story as you hint at the central drama that's about to unfold.

In a moment, we'll take a look at some examples of powerful openings, and then you'll get started writing some of your own. But first, let's examine just what makes for a powerful opening.

Three Main Elements of Powerful Openings

There are three characteristics that I believe are usually present in powerful story openings. Of course there are exceptions—for there are no *absolute* rules in writing, of any kind, at least

Aim to get your
story off to a
roaring start...
by creating as dynamic,
powerful & intriguing
an opening as you can

Caroline Joy Adams

that I like to follow. But, I do think you will find it helpful to keep the following points in mind as you begin to work on your own story concepts.

1. BRING FORTH POWERFUL FEELINGS IN THE FIRST FEW PARAGRAPHS

Whenever you possibly can, it helps to bring forth right from the start strong emotions experienced by the main character—such as frustration, exhilaration, anger, anxiety, anticipation, or any other potent emotions. But there are also times, as in a mystery or suspense story, that the character may be himself unaware of what is about to happen. Yet we, the readers, may be given a *clue* about a dramatic or terrifying situation that's about to take place. In that case, it may then be the reader who experiences a gut-level emotional reaction, perhaps feeling suspense, excitement, terror, fear, or something similar.

But either way, there must be *some* feelings either hinted at or powerfully evoked from the start. And in most cases there should be one or more strong emotions that the reader can easily identify with, that can absorb him or her fully into the drama that's about to unfold.

2. HINT AT THE MAJOR CHALLENGE FACING YOUR MAIN CHARACTER

Some stories begin right in the midst of a highly dramatic situation or with the major conflict explicitly stated. In other cases, the impending conflict is only hinted at and will take time to unravel. But in almost all powerful and effective openings, there is at least a clue about the major crisis, challenge, or conflict that the character will later face—if he or she is not already embroiled in the thick of it.

3. RAISE KEY QUESTIONS ABOUT WHAT'S GOING TO HAPPEN NEXT

Right from the very beginning of any story, unanswered questions should be raised in the mind of the reader. For it's those questions that compel him or her to want to keep reading, to know more, and to satisfy his or her now highly aroused curiosity.

EXAMPLES OF POWERFUL OPENINGS

Now let's look at some powerful openings, keeping in mind that when all three elements are present—that is, when *feelings* are evoked, *conflict* is hinted at, and *questions* are raised—the greater is the potential power to hook your reader from the outset. Following are a few examples, of various lengths: some of my own, some by other writers, including a few that are just one or two paragraphs long.

Real Reason

Stepmother. The very word gave me the creeps, had always made me wince, and I never even knew why. But that May day of my father's wedding, when I was twenty-two years old, and the minister's raspy voice pronounced them man and wife—I got a real, live, official one of my own. And as

my three sisters and I stood there, shifting uncomfortably in
the receiving line to greet the guests, with fake smiles
pasted on our faces, just a scant and unsettling year after
my parents' divorce—I realized I finally had a *real* reason to
hate that word, and all that it stood for.

I chose to open this story with a single word that has great
emotional power—for many of us have an instinctive feeling
about that word, *stepmother.* We may have had difficult experiences of our own, or perhaps we just remember reading
Cinderella as a child.

Let's see if all three elements of powerful openings are present here. The young woman character is clearly feeling these
emotions: hidden anger, resentment, and hatred for her new
stepmother. It is clear, too, that the story will center around
the deep conflict of a family torn apart by divorce and the
personal antagonism that the character feels toward her new
stepmother. Questions are immediately raised, then, as to just
why the young woman has such fierce hatred for her father's
new wife—what has led to this, and what is going to happen
next—arousing the reader's curiosity right from the start. So this
example does meet our criteria for a powerful story opening,
quite effectively.

Now take a look at a few more examples. As you read these
through, note that the intrigue often starts in the first *sentence*—
though in some cases, it builds as the first or second paragraph
flows along.

Through the Night

When I entered the hospital room, as midnight approached, after the long and exhausting five-hour ride—nothing could have prepared me for the intensity of feeling that would flood through me. I was immediately possessed by sharp rays of horror, hope, shock, fear, as I saw my mother lying there helplessly—tubes attached to her everywhere, her skin ghostly white, her life hanging in the balance, not knowing if she'd make it through the night.

As nurses' heels clicked down the hallways, and high-tech machines hummed ominously in the background, I rushed to her side, reached for her limp hand, held it in mine, caressed it softly, and as hot, salty tears slid down my cheeks, whispered hoarsely those words I'd rarely *ever* spoken aloud to her before: "I love you. . . ." And I then silently prayed to God, harder than I'd ever prayed in my life, that she would live—because I couldn't imagine, if she died, how *I* was going to survive, either.

Clearly, in this example, a host of feelings are present. The daughter is full of emotion, including fear, panic, exhaustion, hope, and great anxiety. The conflict is clear, too. The daughter has been called to her mother's side in a hospital, and this truly is a life-or-death drama in process. The major questions raised are whether the mother will live—and if not, how the daughter will handle this, what will her life be like, as she feels losing her mother would be an utter devastation. Thus we are left wondering whether the mother will recover and if this will be the story of a mother's and daughter's ongoing relationship. Or, perhaps it will unfold into a story of an adult daughter coping with her mother's death and her own internal and perhaps dramatic external life changes that result from it.

Here's a third example, and as you read it through, see if *you* can find and identify the three main elements of powerful openings: strong feelings, hints at the major challenge facing the character, and unanswered questions raised.

Just Friends

I felt a queasiness in my stomach, a wave of guilt creeping over me even before I picked up the phone and slowly dialed his number. As it rang, three times, then four, then five, and my hope that he was home, and would answer, escalated, I swallowed hard, and took a sip of the iced ginger ale that was settling, bubbling down, in the tall blue glass I'd just poured for myself. I tried to reassure myself, once again, too, that these late-night calls were totally innocent—that we were "just talking," we were "just friends," anyway. But the truth was that my husband was away, once more, on one of his frequent weeklong business trips—and I didn't miss him a bit. Instead, as usual, it felt freeing, fine, *exhilarating,* to have this brief bit of time to myself—even the bed at night felt so much more comfortable and spacious, too, without his restless, hard-to-please presence.

And though Jeremy and I had not yet crossed any boundaries that were *truly* dangerous—over steaming hot peppermint tea and bites of hot-out-of-the-oven, fresh-baked croissants, and a discussion of our dissertation topics at the nearby university bookstore café on a lovely, warm, misty April afternoon not long ago when the fragrance of lilacs filled the air about campus—we had already confessed our attraction for each other. And we both knew deep down, that it was inexplicable, mysterious, and powerful—and went *way* beyond the physical. But that given the circumstances of our lives, to act on it would be unthinkable indeed. Unless some radical changes took place first—changes we weren't sure that either of us was willing, or ready, to make.

All three keys to a powerful opening are surely present here. The character is experiencing strong feelings, including guilt, longing, and desire for a man other than her husband. The conflict centers around whether or not these two characters will choose to turn their attraction into an illicit affair. The unanswered questions are what will happen if they cannot contain their passionate feelings, and do indeed act on them? Or, what will happen to the woman character if she doesn't indulge her attraction, and chooses instead to wrestle alone with her apparently unhappy marriage?

Now, take a look at another brief, one-paragraph example:

Last Mile

It was a nightmarish ride, two A.M., the wheels were screeching against the rain-drenched pavement as he careened the street corners, every bump in the road pure torture. She writhed in agony, screaming at him, over and over again, to hurry up, sure they'd *never* make it that last mile to the hospital. It felt like the baby was already pushing its way out, like a tornado ripping through a small sieve, pressing against her insides so hard she was sure she'd explode right then and there, and gallons of blood would drench the front seat of the car in no time.

This example also meets the standard for a powerful opening. The character's feelings are clearly very strong: a mix of fear of not making it to the hospital, frustration at the slow ride, and physical agony all at once. The conflict—centering around getting to the hospital on time to have the baby—is evident. We are also left with key unanswered questions—*Will* she make it on time, or will she give birth right then and there? In either case, how is the birth of this baby going to impact the character's life? Obviously, the birth of a child marks a huge transition in any woman's life—and we know that an intriguing and dramatic story is almost certain to follow this powerful opening.

Now, let's look at some openings from some published books and a professional journal. Here's the opening passage to the fiction bestseller of a few years ago, *Mutant Message Down Under*, by Marlo Morgan.

from *Mutant Message Down Under*

It seems there should have been some warning, but I felt none. Events were already in motion. The group of predators sat miles away, awaiting their prey. The luggage I had packed one hour before would tomorrow be tagged "unclaimed" and stay in storage, month after month. I was to become merely one more American to disappear in a foreign country.

This book recounts the tale of an American woman held hostage by a band of Australian Aborigines, based on the author's real-life experience in Australia, with some fictional twists. Clearly, this brief opening paragraph leaves you with a feeling of suspense; makes immediately clear the huge conflict, of the woman being taken prisoner in a foreign land; and raises the questions of just *where* she is, *what* has already happened, and *how* she'll manage to escape this intriguing situation—and come back alive to tell the tale.

Now take a look at the opening to a recent best-selling nonfiction book, *The Gift of Fear.* This is another good example of how nonfiction, just as much as fiction, can open with drama and intrigue and pique our curiosity to the highest degree.

from *The Gift of Fear*

He had probably been watching her for awhile. We aren't sure—but what we do know is that she was not his first victim. That afternoon, in an effort to get all her shopping done in one trip, Kelly had overestimated what she could comfortably carry home. Justifying her decision as she struggled with the heavy bags, she reminded herself that making two trips would have meant walking around after dark, and she was too careful for her safety for that. As she climbed the few steps to the apartment building door, she was aware that it had been left unlatched (again). Her neighbors just don't get it, she thought, and though their lax security annoyed her, this time she was glad to be saved the trouble of getting out her key.

She closed the door behind her, pushing it until she heard the latch. She is certain she locked it—which means he must have *already* been inside the corridor.

In this case, you, the reader, are the one most likely feeling a sense of suspense and tension. And the conflict is obviously that this woman is about to be attacked by a stranger in her own apartment. I would be amazed if you, too, aren't left with a host of unanswered questions: Who he is, what he's planning to do, and what's about to happen to her. The author, Gavin De Becker, has done an excellent job of arousing our interest in the impending drama. I couldn't stop turning the pages of this fascinating book about how our intuition can guide us away from dangerous situations when we are in tune with and listening to it.

Now, read another example of a powerful opening few sentences to a story, which is excerpted from an article I found in a professional magazine called *Family Therapy Networker*.

from "Beauty Resurrected"

Brooklyn, New York, 1957—when doctors still smoked cigarettes while examining their patients in small stuffy

rooms—I was in a hospital, twelve years old, dying. If I
hadn't been fever-crazed I might have known I was dying,
for we were poor, we lived in what was then called "slums."
And what was I doing in a private room, anyway? My family
had no possibility of paying the bill. It was, then, simply
because I was a "charity" case, and with true charity, the
hospital had given me a private room to die in.

This is the start to a powerfully written, lengthy article, with
many autobiographical elements, which somewhat surpris-
ingly evolves into a treatise on the subject of what it is that we
find "beautiful" in our lives. Right from the first sentence, it
evokes a feeling of empathy for the boy and his life situation.
Written by a superb writer and therapist, Michael Ventura,
this opening presents the conflict of a boy from a poor family
who is supposedly about to die. It leaves the reader with the
major question of what's going to happen to this twelve-year-
old boy, too, if he does indeed survive—and how will his true-
life story unfold.

WRITING PRACTICE #3

Now I'd like you to work on creating some one- or two-paragraph
story-starters of your own. So take some time, perhaps give
yourself thirty minutes, and come up with as many two- or
three- or four-*sentence* story-starters as you can in that time.
And remember to aim for your three objectives for a powerful
story opening: evoke *feelings* in your characters and thus in your

readers; make the *conflict* or challenge apparent as you set the stage for your impending drama; and leave your readers intrigued, with *questions* raised that will pique their curiosity to the highest degree.

Here's another approach, too, that you may wish to try. Come up with a few opening sentences or paragraphs with this thought in mind: Once you've gotten to the truly juicy part—*stop*. Stop right *before* he kisses her; or before the car crashes; or before the baby is born; or before the teenaged daughter's father comes barreling into the room catching her with her boyfriend in bed; or whatever the heart of the action is. Then, post some of these brief story-starters on your refrigerator—and look at them during the week. I dare you *not* to write the ending!

And, if you need some topics as starting points for story openers, take a look at the suggested topics following. Keep in mind, too, that your piece doesn't need to be written from your own viewpoint, as a personal experience of your own (called writing in the "first person"—which means using "I" or "we" as pronouns throughout, as you imagine *yourself* to be the main character).

You may be more comfortable describing the experience of other true-to-life or fictional characters, and if so, that's fine. If so, you may wish to use the "third person" viewpoint, which means using pronouns such as "he" or " she" throughout, as you tell the story from an outside *observer's* perspective instead of your own. But whichever viewpoint you use, you can create an equally powerful, interesting opening that has every possibility of leading into an intriguing story.

POSSIBLE TOPICS

- Write about a time when you were in a terrible accident or witnessed one (or when someone you know was in one).

- Write about a time when you realized that you needed to break off a romantic relationship, and focus on either the moment you told the person, or how you agonized ahead of time over how you were going to tell them.

- Write about the best phone call you ever received . . . and what happened as a result.

- Write about the worst phone call you ever received, and how it changed your life immediately.

- Write about a moment when you were in an airport, train or bus station—or on a bus, train, or plane—and met someone new there, or witnessed some dramatic incident.

- Write about a day when you were first aware that you were going to have to make a major life change that you didn't want to make.

- Write about a day when a very close friend told you that they were moving far away . . . or the day they left, and how hard it was to say good-bye.

WRITING PRACTICE #4

Now I'd like you to write several story-starters that are at least two or three paragraphs long. If you feel like writing more, that's fine, too. If you come up with something you like, you may want to expand it into a full-length story, which is what we'll focus on in Keys 3, 4, and 5.

You may also wish to try this exercise—start your story as I did "Stepmother," with just one powerful *word* that has deep meaning for you or to your character. This can be an excellent way to get a story started—and most of the words listed below hold deep associations for many of us. So if it helps, think of one the following thirty words. Allow a dramatic association with it to arise in your mind, and then let the words and story ideas flow.

Mother	Wife	Grandmother
Father	Fiancée	Grandfather
Daughter	Fiancé	Uncle
Son	Lover	Aunt
Sister	Ex-Husband	Boss
Brother	Ex-Wife	Stepsister
Baby	Cousin	Stepbrother
Boyfriend	Doctor	Mother-in-law
Girlfriend	Teacher	Father-in-law
Husband	Lawyer	Neighbor

Writing can be
hard work
but it should also
be PURE FUN
if not always, at least much
of the time!

Caroline Joy Adams

SUMMARY

Key #2: Start Your Story with a Powerful Opening

I hope you had fun with this process, and came up with some intriguing story concepts and interesting story openers of your own. For in almost all cases, powerful stories begin with powerful openings. And there's not much point in writing something that doesn't have a sense of dynamic flow, energy, and power to it. It's just more *fun* to write something that flows along with a high-energy feel—and while writing can be hard work, it should also be pure fun, if not always, at least much of the time!

So go to it, and get your mind spinning off powerful story-starters by the dozens. Once you get started on this track, you may find that they start popping up in your mind at odd moments, at all times of day and night. It's a great way not only to get your mind working creatively, but also to pass the time productively, whenever you're waiting for something or someone. I've gotten in the habit of keeping a pad of clean white, lined paper in my car, so if I arrive at my daughter's school and she gets out late, instead of sitting there feeling annoyed that I'm wasting precious time, I can spin off a few good story-starters. I often find myself totally engrossed in one of them by the time she finally gets in the car, and says, "Mom, let's *go!*"

I then have to say to her, "Now, wait! I'm not ready yet. I just need to get this idea out, a few more sentences, before I forget what I want to say. Just hang on a second!" And I keep scribbling away, till the words I simply *must* get down have all tumbled out, and I've completely forgotten that I was the one waiting for her in the first place.

Create an
Emonional Journey
for Your Reader

Key 3

You're now aware that evoking powerful feelings right from the outset in the character, the reader, or both helps get your story off to a resounding start. But the truth is, you need to *keep* a strong current of feeling flowing throughout the rest of your story. For it's always the underlying *feelings* that fuel a story with momentum, energy, and power—and makes it worth reading from beginning to end. These feelings can cover a wide gamut, even within one relatively short fiction or non-fiction story.

It's always the underlying FEELINGS that fuel a story with momentum, energy & POWER

Caroline Joy Adams

For example, three, four, five, or even more of the following emotions may arise in your characters within one single story: anxiety, alarm, anger, anticipation, or aggravation; fear, frustration, or fury; embarrassment, exhilaration, or elation; hope, heartbreak, or happiness; dismay, dread, or despair; relief, rapture, or resentment; outrage or unease; worry or wistfulness; sorrow, surprise, or suspicion—among countless others. And when your characters are *possessed* by such strong feelings, the reader can connect with and deeply identify with them.

BECOME A TOUR GUIDE FOR YOUR READERS' EMOTIONAL JOURNEY

Your mission, as a writer of a powerful story, is to guide your readers to feel the *same* feelings you are bringing forth in your characters, to invite your readers to feel them, too, at the deepest possible level of their being—emotionally, intellectually, and even physically.

You'll use powerful language, action, description, and sometimes dialogue to accomplish this, and when you succeed in so doing, your reader truly "becomes one" with your characters. That's when they'll come to care about what comes next in the story, too, especially when the specific circumstances the characters find themselves immersed in are far from anything your readers have ever experienced.

So aim, at all times, to infuse your writing with a great variety of feelings—those your readers can relate to and resonate with on all levels—and your readers won't want to put your story down. You'll then know you've created a powerful piece of writing, when you've taken your readers on an *irresistible* emotional journey, all the way through, from the first paragraph to the very last.

Let's look at an example of a very short story, and consider the emotional journey it takes *you,* the reader, on right now.

Twin Souls

He was approaching his eighty-ninth birthday, frail from a serious heart condition that was only getting worse with time; she was eighty-six, and they'd been together practically their entire lives. They'd met one star-filled late June summer night when the roses were in full bloom, had waltzed until the wee hours across a creaky wooden floor to the tunes of Frank Sinatra—and there'd been a heady chemistry between them from the first time he kissed her soft lips goodnight. They'd then spent practically every waking moment together in those precious weeks before he left for his mission aboard the U.S. naval submarine, just as the dreadful events of World War II were beginning to unravel, and forever alter the minds, hearts, and families of so many.

But already deeply in love, and not sure if they'd ever be together again they swore—as they looked into each other's deep blue eyes, tears running down both their cheeks, that bittersweet last night before he took off for Germany—that *if* he came back, they'd marry, in an instant. And never, for any reason, would they be apart from one another again—no matter *what* circumstances life brought their way.

And so it was, after nearly seventy long years of togetherness—that on the second of January, that frigidly cold afternoon after all the holiday festivities were over, when the last of their visiting children and grandchildren had flown home—that they quietly made their way across the wind-swept yard of their neat ranch house to the garage. They then shut the door firmly behind them, turned on the old gray Chevrolet, settled in, locked eyes in a soul-level knowing, reached for each other's hands—and kissed reverently, on the lips one last time, as they allowed the noxious carbon monoxide to fill the room and take over.

It was several days before their neighbor found them— along with the carefully worded hand-written note they'd left, signed by both of them in blue ink, explaining their decision. For at least this way, they'd leave this Earth together, and now nothing—neither time, nor space, nor war, nor sickness—could ever do them part again. For living without each other was not something either of them was willing to do—for a year, a day, or an instant. And even the undertaker had to admit that there was an unusual aura, a look of profound peace, and a sweet, faint smile, on both of their gently wrinkled, and timeworn faces.

I once happened to read an obituary in the local newspaper about a couple who did indeed end their lives by committing suicide together at ages eighty-six and eighty-nine. The newspaper

Your goal is to TRANSPORT your readers out of their ordinary world... taking them on a powerful emotional journey along the way

Caroline Joy Adams

offered few details—but the concept caught my imagination, so I wrote up my own version of who I *imagined* this couple to be, what had happened, and why. (It's a useful writing exercise you might try sometime: take a clipping from a newspaper, flesh it out with added detail, and make of it a much more interesting or dramatic story in your own words.)

For now, though, let's focus on this brief story as an example of the kind of emotional journey you want to create for *your* readers. So let's consider what emotions came up for you as you read this piece.

As you read the first paragraph of "Twin Souls," did you feel a sense of calm and comfort as you imagined a young, dreamy pair who had then gone on to live a long, devoted life together and were now a sweet elderly couple?

Yet as you came to the last sentence of the third paragraph, a moment later—especially when you saw the deadly words *carbon monoxide* and knew what they meant in this context—did you feel startled or dismayed? Did a sense of shock run through you? Were you stunned as you realized that their devotion in life was *so* strong that they had decided to go forward with a mutual suicide pact to avoid what was their worst fear: to live a day on Earth without each other?

As you continued to read through, to the conclusive fourth paragraph, did your own emotions take a little leap forward? Perhaps a sweet sense of relief overcame you, that these two had not, after all, had to endure the hardship of living alone, heartbroken at losing a beloved spouse, as most other elderly men or women do—and as you yourself may fear might happen to you one day?

Clearly, even in an extremely short story, such as this four-paragraph piece, several different emotions can arise. Remember, that's your mission, too, in any story that you tell—to take your reader on a journey to remember, by inspiring a wide range of emotional responses.

Now take a look at one more story example, and as you read, get a sense of what emotions are running through you as your eyes move along the page.

March Morning

Sometimes I still cannot believe that I didn't listen to my intuition that cold March morning, when the wind was whipping like crazy against the windowpanes, rattling them loose, and startling me awake at six o'clock, even before my baby's cries came on. But cry she did, and so I had to force myself out of bed, rescue her from her lonely crib, and try to shush her so she didn't wake my husband, who couldn't stand having to get up before he absolutely had to. But the truth is—I *knew* it, right from that moment, that something wasn't going to be right about that day. A strange, sickening feeling was just there, inside my stomach, like a premonition, I didn't know why, telling me to take it easy, be careful, stay put, maybe not even go out, because if I did— something bad was bound to happen, something I was going to regret.

Even as I left my apartment, then, locking the door

behind me with a loud click, I had the eerie feeling I just should have stayed home. But I couldn't, because this was the day I had an appointment to bring my little Susannah to the clinic for her routine one-year-old checkup. So off I went, practically running the whole ten city blocks to the clinic so I wouldn't be late, pushing the stroller uphill the last three blocks till I was puffing and out of breath, hot and cold jets running through me all at the same time.

But once I arrived, and got inside, away from that fierce wind that had been threatening to blow us over all the way there, with my bright, blue-eyed, eleven-month-old Susannah in tow—I began to feel a little better, and to relax. I could tell, too, that I was in for a long wait—because the crowded waiting room was simply overflowing with women just sitting there, passing the time. Yet still, the easy chatter of other young mothers, whose daily lives were filled with so many of the same joys and burdens as my own, was in the air. I caught snatches of conversations about the same things that floated through my mind all day long—teething troubles, sibling squabbles, marital strains, first words said, and the endless debate as to whether breast-feeding or bottle is best. And while a young baby occasionally squalled, or a restless toddler whined to his mother, "Can't we go *yet?* I wanna go *home* . . . ," all seemed about as ordinary and calm as could be.

Awaiting my turn, to pass the time I began to chat with a talkative young woman who sat beside me. Her name, it turned out, was Delilah, and she had a sweet Southern accent. She told me that she'd just arrived last week from Atlanta, because her fiancé, a young naval officer, had been transferred to the Reserve Station in New York City. And, luckily enough, she went on, she also had an older sister living here, who she was staying with—but whose three-year-old son, Joseph, had just come down with some sort of inexplicable skin rash, and was now being seen by the doctor.

We continued to talk for awhile, about everything and nothing, and then, smiling at my serene, sleeping young daughter, Delilah ventured, "She sure is a cutie. Could I hold her for a just a little bit?" I smiled back at her, proudly, said, "Sure," and as I lifted the baby into her lap, Susannah settled down contentedly without a stir. I went on, "You know, some babies this age can't stand it if anyone holds them but their mother. But not my little Susannah, I'm really lucky, she's just good with *everyone*—grandparents, people in stores, babysitters. . . . She's just got a naturally easygoing, friendly personality. She likes everybody, and everybody likes her. I don't know what I'm going to do, though, when she gets to be a teenager, and all the *boys* like her, too—*then* I'm going to have trouble on my hands, I guess," I laughed, and Delilah smiled back, and chuckled knowingly.

But time was moving on, I was getting restless, my stomach was starting to growl, I was hungry for lunch, my appointment had been scheduled for ten, and yet here it was nearing twelve o'clock. I was starting to feel a wave of sleepiness overtake me, too, due to several night-wakings, and was starting to get mildly annoyed—so I figured I'd ask Delilah if she wouldn't mind keeping an eye on the baby for a second while I went to the receptionist's desk, to find out just how much longer it would be.

But two moments later, when I turned around to head back to my seat, having been told it would only be another ten minutes or so—my heart stopped. My world crashed around me. For Delilah no longer sat in the seat next to where I'd settled in and left my coat and pale pink vinyl baby bag. The hard wooden chairs we'd been sitting on, both of them were now absolutely empty. No trace of Delilah left. And neither was my baby to be seen. She was gone.

I panicked. And heard myself scream louder than I'd ever screamed in my life, "Where *are* they!" But to no avail. No one in the clinic seemed to have noticed a thing. My heart racing, my first instinct told me to just run—as fast as I could, to find them, wherever they were. *Nothing* would stop me, until my beloved only child rested safely in my arms once more.

I then dashed down the long aisle, and out onto the blinding sunlight of Broadway and 168th Street. Crowds of people swarmed by me, buses swerved, taxis blared their loud horns, entrances to the subway lines all blurred before my eyes, as my heart surged. I flagged a policeman, who sympathized, but said he couldn't help me till she'd been gone a certain number of hours, and then could file a missing persons alert.

Furious, I flailed my arms wildly, not knowing which direction to turn in, and stood there, helplessly, in the middle of crowded Broadway, and screamed, once more, at the top of my lungs, "Help! A woman stole my baby! *Where is she?* You've got to help me, someone! Please, please help me, don't let her take my baby!"

Passersby stared at me oddly, some with slight nods of concern, some looks of vague scorn on their faces, thinking I was simply a crazy woman. And I *was* crazed, frozen in that surreal moment in time, with fear, and grief, and guilt for my own stupidity in leaving her, in trusting that woman who I now *knew* was my worst enemy on Earth.

But then—suddenly, I spotted her. She'd been wearing a bright red jacket, and there she was—sauntering across Broadway, holding Susannah, smiling broadly, as if nothing in the world was wrong. She emerged from the thick crowd, ran across the street right toward me, and held my precious angel out for me to take. I grabbed her, held her in my arms with as fierce a love as any mother has ever had. My heart beating wildly, I was about to start raging, "How dare you do this to me! How could you! What were you *thinking!*"

But before the words got out, Delilah was exclaiming chattily, "Oh, she was just *so* adorable, I just couldn't resist, I just simply had to show her to Howard, my boyfriend, 'cause he works so close to here, right down the block from here, at the Naval Reserve! He just *loves* babies, too, and we can't wait to get married and have one of our own! So thanks for letting me borrow her! Sure do appreciate it, honey!"

And with that—she was off, disappearing in a flash, descending into the subway, never to be seen again. I stood there, shocked, relieved, and shaking in disbelief. My worst nightmare had happened. My baby had been taken from me, and worse, it was my own fault. And then, my greatest blessing had happened, almost as quickly—she'd been returned to me.

Forgetting all about the doctor's checkup, I walked the long way home, stopping to take deep breaths all the way—not knowing whether to laugh or cry, or whether I should be more angry or more grateful for what had happened.

But that day I surely learned something I've never let myself forget. That one's world can be turned upside down in an instant—and the course of it perhaps forevermore changed. So to this day, forty-something years later, I have simply thanked the powers that be for the miracle that I did get my beloved daughter back, and have been able to watch her grow into an amazing young woman, who has in turn, through giving birth to two boys of her own, made me a grandmother, now twice over.

And when I look at my grandsons, bright young boys, of varying talents that they are, I can barely imagine what a vastly different life I could and would have had—one marked by unbearable heartache, had my momentary but terrifying loss not been rectified by a triumphant return— that unforgettable cold March morning, now so long ago.

The young mother in this story is my own, and the baby is my older sister. I heard versions of this story many times as I grew up, about a day that could have changed *my* life, as well as everyone else's in my family, forever, had the final outcome been different. And I just recently decided to put it into my own words.

But for a moment, reflect on the various feelings that came up for *you* as you read this story. Did you sense the mother's fear, rage, and helplessness? If so, did it remind you of any times in your life when you've experienced similar emotions? Did it also, perhaps, tug at your own worst fears?

Did you feel a sense of suspense as the story progressed? A sense of relief at the happy ending? Just how many emotional states do you think you shifted into and out of during the five or ten minutes it took you to read through this story?

What I'd like you to be aware of is that even in very short stories, wide ranges of emotions can be brought to the fore. For even in this story of little more than a thousand words, there are a dozen or more feeling states called forth, including the following:

Horror	Guilt	Anticipation
Suspicion	Hesitation	Rage
Suspense	Exhaustion	Confusion
Fear	Frustration	Terror
Worry	Agitation	Gratitude
Dismay	Concern	Shock
Hostility	Alarm	Jubilance
Distress	Anger	Joy

Why Feelings Matter

Feelings, whether in life or in writing, matter so enormously because we human beings, *all* of us without exception, are creatures of feeling. Feelings are the driving force underlying *everything* we do, all that we think, all that we want, all that we hope for, long for, or strive for—and all that we subsequently create of our lives. And we are always feeling *something*—usually a mix of different feelings all at one time. Indeed, whether we are conscious of them or not, most of us go through a huge range of feelings as we progress throughout each day—according to our mood, the people around us, the weather, our state of health, the circumstances we find ourselves in, and so much more. Feelings, then, "logical" or not, are always within us, bubbling under the surface, in great variety and abundance.

When we take the time to read a story, too, it's almost always because we are hoping to have an emotional experience, often one that will distract us from what we are already feeling. And we read because we want to *change* our emotional state. If we happen to be bored when we pick up a book or magazine, we may hope to get a rush of adrenaline by reading an exciting story. If we are agitated, annoyed, or angry, we'll look for something amusing, funny, perhaps spiritually uplifting, to calm our emotional fires. Then again, if we are feeling sad, we may want to read something—whether it's dramatic or light-hearted—that will take our minds off our own troubles.

Yet we rarely take the time to consider—in life and in writing—the many different feelings that can overtake us. Most of us are never taught to clearly identify the feelings we are immersed in at any given moment; this is one reason psychotherapists have such an important role to play in our society and have such a huge potential market. For the major focus of therapy is often to help adults sort through the feelings they were never allowed to identify, or fully experience, as children.

But in any case, our job as writers is to consciously infuse the characters in our stories with feeling. I believe, too, that it can be helpful to develop an enhanced awareness of the great variety of feeling states that we might bring out in our characters. With this in mind, I offer you a list of 250 or so words that describe both "negative" and "positive" feeling states, ones that we all experience at times.

Some of these words may find their way into your stories, giving the reader a more specific sense of the character's state of mind. But for the most part, just think of this list as a reference tool that can help you become clear about which emotional states you want to emphasize and call forth in your characters—and subsequently in your readers.

For the deeper and more emotionally complex your characters, the more realistic and intriguing they will be to your readers. As you envision your characters, then, and move them through your story line, ask yourself which emotional states they are most likely to possess, given who they are and the circumstances you are immersing them in. Be sure, then, that you make these feelings apparent to your readers, whether through dialogue, which reveals the characters' spoken or interior thoughts, or through other clues or forms of description.

"NEGATIVE" WORDS TO DESCRIBE EMOTIONS THAT YOUR CHARACTERS MAY BE FEELING

afraid	deadened	fearful
aggravated	dejected	fidgety
agitated	depressed	forlorn
alarmed	despairing	frightened
aloof	despondent	frustrated
angry	detached	furious
anguished	disaffected	gloomy
annoyed	disenchanted	guilty
anxious	disappointed	harried
apathetic	discouraged	heavy
apprehensive	disheartened	helpless
aroused	dismayed	hesitant
ashamed	displeased	horrible
beat	distressed	horrified
bewildered	disturbed	hot
bitter	disquieted	humdrum
blah	downcast	hurt
blue	downhearted	impatient
bored	drained	indifferent
brokenhearted	dull	intense
chagrined	edgy	irate
cold	embarrassed	irked
concerned	embittered	irritated
confused	exasperated	jealous
cool	exhausted	jittery
cross	fatigued	keyed-up

lazy	puzzled	terrified
leery	rancorous	tired
lethargic	reluctant	troubled
listless	repelled	uncomfortable
lonely	resentful	unconcerned
mad	restless	uneasy
mean	sad	unglued
miserable	scared	unhappy
mopey	sensitive	unnerved
morose	shaky	unsteady
mournful	shocked	upset
nervous	skeptical	uptight
nettled	sleepy	vexed
numb	sorrowful	weary
overwhelmed	sorry	wistful
panicky	spiritless	withdrawn
passive	startled	woeful
perplexed	surprised	worried
pessimistic	suspicious	wretched
powerless	tepid	

"POSITIVE" WORDS TO DESCRIBE EMOTIONS THAT YOUR CHARACTERS MAY BE FEELING

absorbed	animated	awestruck
adventurous	angelic	blissful
affectionate	appreciative	breathless
alert	ardent	buoyant
alive	aroused	calm
amazed	astonished	carefree
amused	awed	charged-up

cheerful	fulfilled	peaceful
comfortable	glad	perky
complacent	gleeful	pleasant
composed	glorious	pleased
concerned	glowing	powerful
confident	good-humored	proud
contented	grateful	quiet
cool	gratified	radiant
curious	happy	rapturous
dazzled	helpful	refreshed
delighted	hopeful	relaxed
eager	inquisitive	satisfied
ebullient	inspired	secure
ecstatic	intense	sensitive
effervescent	interested	serene
elated	intrigued	spellbound
enchanted	invigorated	splendid
encouraged	involved	stimulated
energetic	joyous	surprised
engrossed	joyful	tender
enlivened	jubilant	thankful
enthusiastic	keyed-up	thrilled
excited	loving	touched
exhilarated	mellow	tranquil
expansive	merry	trusting
expectant	mirthful	upbeat
exultant	moved	warm
fascinated	optimistic	wide-awake
free	overjoyed	wonderful
friendly	overwhelmed	zestful

Through a heightened awareness of feeling states, invite your readers into the minds and lives of your characters. You may note that there are more "negative" emotional states mentioned here than "positive" ones. But that's because in writing, as in real life, it's the negative states—those associated with our challenges and conflicts—that have the most emotional force and staying power for us. So, incorporate them both in your writing, when appropriate, of course. Remember, too, that the journey you provide for your reader should be an enthralling, emotionally gripping, and ultimately fulfilling one, whether your story has a happy or a tragic ending. Always hold it as your intention to lead your readers along and offer them a true, action-packed emotional experience. And with that in mind, let's get started writing!

WRITING PRACTICE #5

I'd now like you to write a short story from start to finish. It can be as short as a page or two, or as long as you like. Just make sure there's an interesting main character who feels a variety of powerful feelings that are appropriate to the action, and at least one central conflict that leads to a resolution.

In most cases, your character will progress through at least three (or more) emotional states. As you contemplate the emotional journey you'd like to provide for your reader, ask yourself these questions: What are at least three emotions that your main character is *likely* to pass through as the events of your story unfold? For example, is the main character likely to experience fear, suspense, and relief? Or exhilaration, anger, and calm? Or sorrow, hope, and joy? Or other emotions altogether?

Be clear which emotions will make for the most compelling story, and consciously focus on bringing them out as you write.

Always ask yourself, too, if there is anything more you can do to ensure that your readers sense the characters' emotions— thus arousing their own emotions to the highest degree in the process.

If it helps, after you are done with a story, go back over it, look at it closely, and make a list (taken from our list of 250 negative and positive feeling-state words) of *all* the emotional states you've included. This can be an excellent way to assess whether you've created enough of a variety of realistic emotions to keep your readers emotionally involved and absorbed. Here are some possible new story topics to get you started.

POSSIBLE TOPICS

- ⬿ Write a story that begins with a scene where you were feeling elated, but then something happened to make you sad, furious, or extremely frustrated.

- ⬿ Write a story that begins with a scene when you (or your characters) had a truly terrible blind date . . . and perhaps went from feeling happy and hopeful to disappointed or annoyed or worse, in a matter of moments.

- ⬿ Write a story that begins with a scene when you were so angry that you couldn't help expressing it in public, much to your great embarrassment later.

↜ Write a story that begins with a scene when you (or your characters) are experiencing a moment of extreme embarrassment, or when you (or they) are forced to confront one of your (or their) worst fears.

WRITING PRACTICE #6

Now come up with another story topic and write another story altogether—even if it's just a few pages. Make a concerted effort, this time, to call forth an entirely *different* set of emotional states in your characters (and your readers) than you did in Writing Practice #5. For instance, if your previous story focused on emotional states such as fear, suspense, and relief, now write a story revolving around the emotions of sorrow, hope, and a renewed sense of joy—or pick another set of emotional states altogether.

The point is to exercise your own "emotional writing muscles" by expanding your awareness of emotional states in yourself and in your characters, for this can infuse much more emotional power into your writing. It can make for a much richer, fuller storytelling experience for you, as the writer, as well as for those who get to read the final result of your efforts.

Once you KNOW
what the STORY is
& get it right...
right as you can, anyway...
it belongs to anyone who
wants to read it...

Stephen King

SUMMARY

Key #3: Create an Emotional Journey for Your Reader

The *motion* of emotion is what fuels powerful writing and keeps it moving rapidly along. Remember, too, that your stories, short or long, funny or deeply dramatic, are offerings to your readers to take them on an emotional journey, allowing them to end up in a different place than where they started. That's what they are actively seeking through the written word, too: to be transported from their ordinary world and current emotional state into another—and *you* have the power to create that experience for them.

Whether fact or fiction, stories may not have happy endings. But even so, there is always a sense you've come to *some* satisfactory stopping place. For poignant or highly dramatic, harrowing or humorous, in any given story you write you are taking your readers on an emotion-packed ride, where they will shift gears at least a few times, from high to low and back again. And you *must* leave them with their curiosity about the central intrigue satisfied, and their emotions having been through a workout that now feels complete in some way.

Invite the whole wide spectrum of emotional states into your writing, allowing them to become the underlying current that shoots exciting rays of energy into all that occurs in your stories. For this is what allows us to fully feel what your characters are feeling—and to become *one* with them, heart, mind, and soul, for the duration of the marvelous journey of words you've invented and are inviting us to participate in.

Ask the Six Most Important Questions About Your Unfolding Story

Key

4

IF YOU WORKED ON THE suggested Writing Practices of Key #3, you've now had some practice writing at least two complete stories. And I bet once you read them over, you were satisfied with *some* aspects of your stories, but at the same time you may have felt that other aspects could be strengthened. There are nearly always things that, once we read our work, we may want to do differently. And that's what the revision process is about. This step can, of course, be just as fun and creative as writing the original draft—even though it may *also* seem to be where the hard work of writing comes in.

The truth is that very few of us can write a "perfect" story, fiction or nonfiction, the first time out. Much more likely we'll need to re-read and refine what we've written—sometimes several times, until it reads smoothly, logically, and powerfully all the way through. And that's just what we'll be working on in this chapter.

How I Write My Own Stories

First, though, I'd like to share with you some of what I do as I write my own stories—which may help you think through your own initial process.

My stories usually are triggered by a real-life memory, which I then take off with and which frequently leads into a much more fictional version of the subject or scene. And I must say that this often takes me by total surprise. I start by thinking I am going to write a fairly true-to-life version of what happened. Yet somehow, the creative instinct takes over, and before I know it I am flying off into the realm of pure imagination.

What seems to happen most often is that I get carried away by a *feeling* that was evoked for me by the memory of the scene that has arisen in my mind. And that feeling—whether it's sadness, anger, wistfulness, frustration, exhilaration, or any other emotion—often finds its way into the mind, body, and heart of one of the characters in the story, and takes them places I may never even have *imagined* when I first set pen to paper.

And as you'll note in the examples that I have included so far, most of my characters seem to be wrestling with huge life crises or issues concerning difficult or challenging situations or relationships with parents, children, lovers, or spouses. That's what interests me the most in life and in writing, so it's no surprise that I find it easy and fun to write about such emotional topics.

I know, too, that I get fired up and *want* to write the rest of the story when I get to the heart of the conflict right from the start. So I do try to follow my own advice about beginning with a powerful opening line or paragraph.

If I have time, I like to write the entire story in one sitting, the whole way through, allowing it to flow out however it comes. It's then that I can go back over it and ask the questions that can help me clarify what I need to change, add, or delete to make for a stronger story.

And while at times I make a careful outline first and try to stick to it, once I get going, I find I often take off in a somewhat different direction than planned, and frequently the ending takes me by total surprise.

You may find that you work differently—perhaps you find it best to outline a story first and stick to a planned plot. If that works for you, especially if your stories recount your own true-life experiences, that's fine. But if you do take this approach, it's always good to be flexible as you go along—allowing for spontaneity and for the creative flow to take its own natural course. For this, to me, is a huge part of the *fun* of writing.

In either case—whether you have a clear idea what your

Always be
OPEN, flexible
& spontaneous...

Allow your story to take YOU
by surprise, & to unfold in a
totally different direction
than you may have expected...

Caroline Joy Adams

story is going to be about, or whether the story unfolds one line, paragraph, and page at a time—it always helps to go back over your writing once you do have a first draft, and ask yourself some key questions.

These questions will help you assess the strengths and weaknesses in your story; give you a sense as to whether your story is heading in the right direction and possesses enough emotional staying power; and help you determine what you may want to do differently as you rework and refine your story.

THE SIX QUESTIONS

These are the questions that journalists (who are attempting to include all the *facts* in a story) usually ask themselves. But the questions can be just as useful when you are writing fiction—or an interplay between fact and fiction, as is often the case in my own writing, and perhaps in yours, too.

These six questions are meant to help you determine

- *What* the main conflict of your story is;

- *Who* your characters are;

- *When* your story takes place;

- *Where* your story takes place;

- *How* the events that lead up to the story's beginning may have contributed to the drama of the opening scene; and

- *Why* this story is worth telling, why the characters are driven to take the actions they are about to take.

85

Let's go over each question in greater detail.

1. WHAT IS THE MAIN THEME OF THE STORY, THE CENTRAL CONFLICT OR PROBLEM YOUR CHARACTERS ARE CONFRONTED WITH?

As you are now well aware, you must, preferably within the first page of your story, present a conflict—a problem, difficult situation, or circumstance—that confronts the main character. It can be useful to define this challenge in one brief sentence or two, also—for this helps you gain clarity about the essential theme of your story.

Using "March Morning" as an example: "This story is about a young mother whose baby was suddenly kidnapped, and her desperate search to retrieve her only child." That's a concise, accurate, and simple way to describe the main theme.

Now, let's go back to the other example of Key #3, my brief story called "Twin Souls." Here's a quick summary of that plot: This story is about an elderly couple, married for nearly seventy years, who feel so deeply connected they cannot bear the thought of living without each other; so in order to avoid the terrible trauma of having one of them die first, leaving the other in a state of loss and grieving, they choose to die together in a mutual suicide pact.

But even if your story is a much longer one, you'll still find it helps if you can briefly sum up its main theme. To that end, I include a few examples of quick plot synopses of some recent *New York Times* fiction bestsellers, as follows:

One Door Away from Heaven, by Dean Koontz. This is a story about a woman who is attempting to protect a nine-year-old girl from her stepfather, a man who is somehow convinced that her destiny revolves around UFOs and space aliens.

Skipping Christmas, by John Grisham. A married couple discovers that their difficult decision to do away with Christmas this year comes with serious, unexpected consequences.

Basket Case, by Carl Hiassen. A journalist living in South Florida becomes obsessed with investigating the strange circumstances surrounding the death of a famous rock musician.

The Corrections, by Jonathan Franzen. This revolves around a mother who has attempted to bring her highly dysfunctional family, of various generations, together for a final Christmas celebration at home.

The Millionaires, by Brad Meltzer. Two brothers who work at an exclusive bank attempt to pull off a foolproof crime, but their plans go astray.

Smoke in Mirrors, by Jayne Anne Krentz. After her death, the last attempted scam of a woman known to be something of a con artist and seductress comes back to haunt one of her dearest friends.

Thursday's Child, by Sandra Brown. This story revolves around an identical twin, a scientist, who pretends to be her very opposite sister, goes on a date, and ends up in a complex romantic entanglement.

Now, here are a few plot summaries of nonfiction bestsellers:

Bias, by Bernard Goldberg. This is a story told from the viewpoint of a television reporter who worked at a major network,
informing us how "the media distorts the news."

The Final Days, by Barbara Olson. An interesting tale of "the
last, desperate abuses of power" in the White House, written by a conservative news commentator, who sadly enough
died aboard one of the hijacked jetliners of September 11.

Every Breath You Take, by Ann Rule. This story tells the dramatic
true life-and-death tale of Sheila Bellush, whose former husband, Allen Blackthorns, a millionaire, apparently paid to
have her killed.

The point here is that it's important for you to be as clear as
possible about your main theme—whether you are writing a
two-paragraph story or a longer one that will have many twists
and turns along the way. So do take time after you've written
your first draft, and see if you can come up with an accurate,
telling one-liner, summing up and describing the essential story
line. If you try this, I think you'll have a much better sense of
the true focus of your story. Then, when you go back in for a
second round to make changes and sharpen things up, you'll
be able to hone in easily on what's *most* important to your
unfolding story.

2. WHO IS THE STORY ABOUT?

Let's not forget that all stories are essentially about *people.* Thus,
your characters are of paramount importance in defining your

Stories are essentially about PEOPLE & their dreams, desires & dramas... So make your characters as compelling as possible, so your readers will come to care about what happens to them ...

Caroline Joy Adams

story line. As the writer, then, you need to have an accurate, detailed, deep sense of who your main characters are and what it is about them that *you* find unique or intriguing—so you can be sure to convey this to your readers. Take time to think through all the different aspects of your characters' personalities. Then, present details that make those characteristics apparent, realistic, and interesting.

And while there are often multiple characters in a story, there is nearly always one main character whose heart, mind, and body, we "borrow" for the story's duration, whose skin we need to "step inside," if the story is to become real for us. This is true for almost all short stories: fiction or nonfiction. (In *novels,* there can be several main characters, and we may be given glimpses of their interior workings through alternating chapters that are told through each character's viewpoint.)

As your main character makes his or her way through the difficult circumstances at hand, he or she will experience a wide range of emotions. It's up to you to pull your reader into feeling those very same feelings, right along with your character. And it helps if your main character is someone your readers can empathize with, someone they can relate to, they will be silently rooting for, and they hope *will* overcome the challenges at hand (even while there are, most likely, other thoroughly dislikable characters in the story, who perhaps are the cause of, or embroiled somehow in, the conflict).

Let's go back to "March Morning" as an example. The main character is clearly the young mother—and it's her feelings we are resonating with, and living with, all the way through. We know enough to get a picture of her in our mind—and most women readers (especially those who are mothers themselves) will certainly empathize with her feelings, including her shock and terror when her child is taken from her.

So be sure that *you* have a clear sense of who your characters are, what makes them interesting and unique, and what they are thinking, feeling, and wanting all the way through your story. And as you read over your story, if your characters don't seem "real" enough, go back in and add details that will flesh them out and reveal deeper layers of who they are. Let us in on their inner workings as much as you can—for this is one of the keys to creating stories that your readers will relate to, resonate with, and want to read, over and over again.

3. WHEN IS THE STORY TAKING PLACE?

Time, of course, is a crucial element of all stories. It's important to establish the historical time period in which your story is set if this has a major effect on the story line. It's also helpful to give a sense of the time of year or time of day a story is taking place in: the season, month, day of the week, or time of day or night. You may need to give us a sense of the ages of the characters involved. Some stories, too, take place over a wide range of time, spanning, say, sixty years, with various scenes providing flashbacks to earlier moments in the character's life.

Inevitably, then, you will be making references to time, answering the "*When* is this happening?" question at various points throughout your story. For example, in "March Morning," right away it is clear that the action is occurring in the month of March. We know that it's morning and that the scene in the doctor's waiting room revolves around a sense of frustration on the part of the main character, that she is being forced to wait too long to see the doctor, making time seem to pass too slowly.

Yet once the child is missing, time seems to speed up. And, then it seems to slow down again as the character races around trying to find the missing baby and her kidnapper. The phrase, "frozen in that surreal moment of time," indicates that terrible moment, too, when the young mother feels most desperate and helpless. But by story's end, we find out that *this* moment in time, this memorable day, actually took place forty years earlier—and our perspective then shifts to the present reality of an elderly grandmother recounting a tale from her youth.

Be sure, then, that you continually use words that allow your readers to gain a clear sense of *when* your scenes are taking place. This can have a huge effect on the overall sense of continuity and flow of your story. As well, it can add key elements of surprise, perhaps at the ending, when we find that we are in fact looking at scenes from the character's past, through the lens of time gone by.

4. WHERE IS THE STORY SET?

Where your story takes place is also important information to the reader. You may, of course, portray many different settings and scenes in one story. In "March Morning," the story starts with the woman waking up in her bedroom; then we are given a brief image of her leaving her apartment and locking the door. Then she is walking outside, rushing to get to the clinic. So, there are three different settings presented right there within the first half-page of the story.

Next, the young mother arrives at the clinic, and time passes for a while in that setting, as the true drama sets in, and she rushes wildly out the door of the clinic into the streets in the mad search to find her missing daughter. The street scene is vividly portrayed in a sentence: "Crowds of people swarmed by me, buses swerved, taxis blared their horns, entrances to the subway all blurred before my eyes as my heart surged. . . ."

The next setting is when she is walking home once more, "stopping to take deep breaths all along the way." Within this short story, then, there are at least five separate "scenes," or settings. Your stories may have many more, or perhaps less. But in any case, be sure that you always answer the question of *where* your characters are at any given time.

It's also useful to note that the *When* and *Where* questions are often deeply intertwined in a story. Referring back to "Twin Souls," we are given a glimpse of several settings, answering the "Where?" question, starting with the dance where the young couple met; then we see an image of them parting before the war; and next, there's the scene in the garage as they end their lives together. These last two scenes are portrayed as sixty years apart—yet they lead easily into each other, through a key transitional sentence, making it immediately apparent how much time has passed.

Remember to indicate, then, whenever possible, the most

telling and interesting features of *where* your drama is taking place—especially if it ties heavily into *when*. This will add enormously to the whole impact of the story, satisfying your readers' need to know both where and when your action is set.

5. HOW DID THIS STORY COME TO TAKE PLACE? WHAT ARE THE LIFE EVENTS THAT HAVE LED UP TO THE STORY'S OPENING SCENE?

There are times when a few sentences at the beginning of a story can give the reader a sense of how events leading up to the story's opening may affect what is about to happen. For instance, in "March Morning," we are given the sense right away that the main character is a mother who is about to take her baby for a doctor's visit. We can assume that she has been planning this visit for awhile; we most likely know, too, that it's normal to take a baby for a routine one-year-old checkup. And we can likely identify with her sense that it's hard to feel justified in canceling such an appointment just because she has a "bad feeling" inside that something might happen.

This information gives us a brief but important sense of what has likely taken place beforehand, and sets the stage for what's going to happen next. In other stories, much more information may be needed at a story's beginning before it can lead to the central action, conflict, or drama. But always make clear, even in a few phrases, sentences, or pages, how previous events in the characters' lives have laid the groundwork for what is about to unfold.

6. WHY DO THE CHARACTERS WANT TO TAKE THE ACTIONS THEY ARE TAKING?

Whether your story stems from real life or pure fiction, it is always important that the characters feel *real* to your reader. The characters' actions may border on the mysterious, hard to fathom, or utterly outrageous—but there needs to be *some* motivation for them nonetheless. In "March Morning," the mother's actions—taking the child to the doctor, then doing everything in her power to find her baby once she's missing— clearly stem from her love, sense of devotion, and desire to protect her child. It's the motivation of the other major character, Delilah, however, that comes as a shock and surprise in the end.

And the truth is, of course, that people, in real life and in fiction, are vastly complicated. Sometimes we don't even understand our own motivations. Yet there is always some driving force behind everything that we do and that we make our characters do, whether it's to demonstrate our love for another; to gain fame, fortune, money, power, or possessions; to get revenge; or to clumsily attempt to create a sense of human connection, even at times through the wrong use of brute force. So be sure that you have some sense as to why your characters are engaging in the course of action that they are taking—or your readers won't be able to make sense of your story, either.

Also, ask yourself the other basic "Why?" question: Why are you telling *this* story, among all the other story possibilities that exist? Does it truly feature characters that your readers will resonate with? Does it contain an intriguing enough situation and story line to capture the imagination of your readers?

Not every story has to appeal to everyone, of course; indeed certain stories will appeal only to one segment of the population: say, young mothers, or single women looking for romance, or men who are sports or history fanatics, or those enthralled with mysteries or science fiction or fantasy.

There really is no such thing as a story that everyone will want to read, resonate with, love, or even like. But as long as you know that *someone* else will likely find your story worth reading, go ahead, write it, polish it, and do whatever you can to make it as powerful a read as possible.

Using the Six Questions

If you ask these six key questions of yourself and apply them to your stories, you will determine whether you've left out any important information. If so, you can go back and add it in. This will greatly enhance the possibility that your story reads clearly and will sustain the reader's interest. For the last thing you want is a reader who's lost, confused, bored, or restless, struggling to understand what's happening or where the story is going.

Instead, you want to get your readers as emotionally involved in your characters' life dramas and crises as possible from the get go. And when you can answer these six questions clearly for *yourself,* you undoubtedly will succeed in doing so for your readers, too. So now, let's get some more writing underway!

WRITING PRACTICE #7

Now, write a new, complete short story. Or, you may choose to go back over the story you wrote for Writing Practice #5 or #6 and rework it a bit.

Either way, after you've written your story, go back over it, and ask yourself the *What, Who, How,* and *Why* questions about your story. If you find that there is anything that has not been made as clear as possible to the reader about the characters—such as their motivations—then make these changes, to add clarity, energy, power, and direction to your story.

Ask yourself, too, if the conflict is clear—and if not, what you can do to strengthen it, perhaps by giving more hints about what led up to the story's opening scene. Go back in, paragraph by paragraph, and see where such changes could be made. Then add them in.

WRITING PRACTICE #8

Now go back over the story you just wrote, and be sure that you are answering the *When* and *Where* questions. Count the number of settings you've described. Are there too many? Too few? If it would help to condense and eliminate some, see if you can do so. If it might add interest to add additional locations, then make that change, too.

Or consider if there are any other compelling details you've left out about the setting that might just add zest, zing, and intrigue to your story. Indicate, whenever possible, the *most*

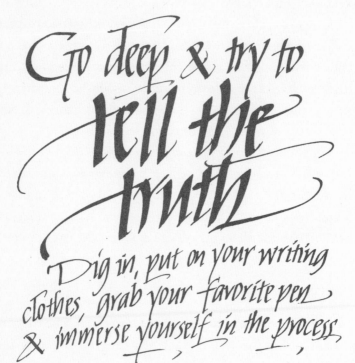

Go deep & try to
**tell the
truth**

Dig in, put on your writing
clothes, grab your favorite pen
& immerse yourself in the process.

Eric Maisel

telling and interesting features of where your drama is taking place. This will add enormously to the whole impact of the story, satisfying your readers' need to know where your action is set.

Then, ask yourself if the *time sequence* is always clear, or if any changes are needed to ensure that your readers clearly grasp the sense of time in which the story takes place and that any use of flashbacks to earlier times is done in a clean and clear way. Then make any changes that are needed.

SUMMARY

Key #4: Ask the Six Most Important Questions About Your Unfolding Story

Interesting stories always have as their basis the posing and answering of questions for the readers, such as,

- ☙ Who is this character?

- ☙ Why should I care about him?

- ☙ What's going to happen to him if I keep turning the pages?

And, perhaps most important,

- ☙ Is this story going to be satisfying, entertaining, comforting, surprising, or thrilling—and worth the time it takes to read?

Questions abound and are hugely important. For like feelings, they are the driving force behind all that happens in our lives. So use the *power of questions* as you write—especially those key six *What, Who, When, Where, How,* and *Why* questions—to be sure you are giving your readers the richest, most powerful reading experience you're capable of producing. Answer the questions for yourself, too, as you rewrite, by adding details when they are helpful to the reader's understanding of the story. And that is what we'll focus on in Key #5 of *The Power to Write.*

Part II

Continue to Develop and Refine Your Writing Skills

Focus on the Five Senses: Sight, Sound, Taste, Scent, and Touch

Key 5

IT'S NOW TIME TO FLESH OUT your stories with descriptive, sensory details, which can add real power, zest, life, and energy to your characters, the settings in which they find themselves, and your unfolding drama.

Sensory details are critical to powerful writing because they can set a mood; evoke a huge array of feelings; trigger memories for both your character or your readers; and draw them into *believing* that they are right there, in that scene, in that moment, inside your character's mind.

Description
composed of sensory detail
PENETRATES layers
of consciousness, engaging
your reader emotionally
as well as intellectually...

Rebecca McClanahan

Visual descriptions are most common, but it's enormously helpful to include, in every piece of writing, some details of the other senses—sound, taste, scent, and touch. These additional sensory details can help bring the scene to life and make it as three-dimensional an experience as possible for your reader.

The Power of Sensory Detail

In real life (assuming you are blessed with the full possession of all five of your senses), you are constantly awash in sensory experience. You may not be consciously aware of all of them, but you are surrounded, in every single moment, by a vast variety of sights, sounds, scents, and potential taste and touch sensations. So let's now consider each of these five senses briefly.

1. SIGHT

For most of us, visual images predominate our awareness. No matter where we are, we see what's happening around us, from our own image in the mirror to the faces of those around us, as we speak to our loved ones, coworkers, or friends—from the streets of our neighborhood to the familiar landscapes we take in as we drive to work. We also see countless images flashing across television screens each day, as well as numerous photographic images that grace the pages of the newspapers or magazines we read.

From the interiors of the office buildings or malls or supermarkets that make up part of our daily landscape to the welcome-home smile of our child or spouse at night, it is literally impossible to count the sheer number of different images we see in a day. And this is one reason why we usually only take notice of the *most* memorable and important visual details of our surroundings, for to take it all in would be overwhelming.

The same, then, should be true of the visual details you include in your writing. Offer your readers details of a setting's or character's looks that are the *most* interesting, relevant, telling, and compelling—and leave out those details that do not increase the feeling of intrigue or further the reader's understanding of the characters and their conflicts.

2. SOUND

We are also immersed, in real life, in a continuous sea of sound. In a given day, at the very least, a few dozen different sounds are present in our environments. These may include the sound of our own breathing as we wake from a deep sleep first thing in the morning; water gushing from a faucet; horns blaring and other traffic sounds; music of all sorts, which if it's discordant may grate on our nerves and make us feel angry or agitated, or, if it's to our liking may make us feel like dancing or singing along, instantly elevating our mood, making us happier, more relaxed, and energized.

Our sound-environment may also include computers or other appliances humming in the background of our homes or offices; clinking plates and glasses at a restaurant; babies crying; animals, such as cats meowing or dogs barking; the sounds of voices speaking, pleasant and loving and soft at times, harsh or shrill at other times; and so much more.

If we *really* listened, and made a list of the sounds we hear in a given day, we'd almost certainly find it's far more than we'd expect. And most of those sounds we do need to tune out, in order to focus on what's most essential from moment to moment.

But when we write, and selectively incorporate even two or three sound elements into our *stories,* such as an alarm bell going off; a car screeching to a halt on wet pavement; a dish falling to the floor and shattering into a thousand tiny fragments—great power can be added to a scene. So do attempt to introduce details of sound into the action of your story, and you may be surprised at how easily and effectively this can enliven and empower your writing.

3. TASTE

We experience a wide variety of taste and scent sensations every day, and store hundreds or even thousands in our memory banks, associated with specific times and places, all of which can instantly evoke certain feelings in us. And, of course, the twin senses of taste and scent are often (though not always) intertwined.

We all look forward to eating or drinking several times a day (not just to ease our hunger pangs), so we can enjoy a variety of taste sensations: from fresh-out-of-the-oven bread, banana muffins, or chocolate cake; to hot sizzling steak; to richly spiced, tangy tomato sauce; to a cold glass of sugary iced tea with a generous slice of lemon on a scorching hot summer's day. These taste sensations, like many others, have powerful and pleasant associated scents—and can bring up key memories for us, or for our characters, in the right circumstances—just as unpleasant tastes and scents can bring raw emotional power to a scene when there are negative connotations to such sensations.

4. SCENT

Scent alone can have as much power on the written page as do combined scent/taste sensations. For there are many scents that do not have associated tastes: the mesmerizing summery scent of roses, lilacs, or other potent freshly bloomed flowers; the thick smoke from a roaring fire; the strong scent of pine trees in the woods; the musty smell of a dog that has just come in from a night out in the rain, and many others.

It's not always crucial, or even possible, to mention details of scent and taste in your stories—but when you *can* incorporate even one or two such details, it can add an important element of realism and bring your scene to life more vividly for your reader.

5. TOUCH

Touch has been called the "mother of all the senses," for right from the moment we are born it is the touch of our mother's body against our own that provides us with an instant sense of comfort, connection, and nurturance—even while our eyes are shut tight and visual imagery does not yet exist for us.

Touch, indeed, is vitally important for our physical, emotional, and mental well-being, and those who are deprived of enough nurturing touch, at any age, may suffer greatly as a result. Since it is such a vital part of life, it's surely worth trying to introduce touch sensations into your writing—even though it may seem hard to describe such physical sensations through words on paper.

But whenever you can, give us a glimpse not only of how your characters feel *emotionally*, but of how they are feeling *physically*, too. So include details of the sensations their skin feels when touched in various ways: by the weather or air temperature, which may either soothe them or cause them discomfort; by another person's touch, which may thrill, comfort, or repel them; or by a texture, pleasing or annoying, that their skin comes into contact with.

Give us details of how your character may be roasting hot as he sits watching a baseball game on a sweltering summer day; or cold and chilled to the bone on a damp winter day as she waits outside for a bus that's way too late in coming; or itchy from a scratchy sweater; or agitated because of shoes that are too tight; or thrilled because his lover, away on a long business trip, has returned, and he can now feel the passionate heat of her touch that he's been constantly craving while alone.

At times, too, describe textures that may be pleasing as your character comes in contact with them: a silky pillowcase that provides comfort even as she cries into it late at night after a terrible romantic breakup; a rich, thick velvet jacket that makes her feel more confident as she heads for a job interview she is nervous about; a newborn baby's ivory-smooth face the very first time he touches it; the exquisitely delicate, soft petals of a flower that she finds in the woods—or anything else that feels like something that we, too, have felt and can completely and vividly imagine feeling in that moment.

CREATE DYNAMIC, MOVING "WORD PICTURES"

So as you write, or rewrite, your story, be as generous as possible with your sensory, descriptive details. For your essential task is to paint what you may think of as a gorgeously rendered "word picture" for your reader. Think of this as a dynamic, *moving* picture, too. Include details that help us get to know the characters, their feelings, moods, and motivations; that evoke feelings; that move the action along; and that give us clues about important unfolding events. Describe sights, sounds, scents, and taste and touch sensations *whenever* such details allow us to imagine a more vivid, realistic scene—and your story will be enormously enriched. So now, let's look at how sensory details are used in a few examples:

Birth Night

It was the ninth of August, and the small upstairs bedroom was hot, humid, permeated with the damp, musky smell of the sweat dripping off all of our foreheads, and soaking through our summer T-shirts, as we gathered around her, all of us exhausted by then—for what we hoped would now be the final, triumphant push to the finish. And within moments there he was, after those sixteen long drawn-out hours, emerging, fully, at last.

Offer your readers
the MOST
compelling details...
calling forth each of the
five senses, whenever possible...

Caroline Joy Adams

But we could immediately see that the cord was
wrapped tightly around his neck like a noose, his eyes shut
tight, his mouth set in a frown, his face deeply wrinkled
like a very old and unhappy man, his face purplish—blue
in color, his tiny body blood-streaked and completely
unmoving. My wild-eyed nine-year-old nephew, there to
witness the birth of his baby brother jumped up and
screamed out in panic, "He looks like he's dead!"

This describes the night that my now teenage nephew was
born. It was a home birth, at my sister's house, with various
friends and family members present, and was a highly dramatic event indeed.

Four senses—all but taste—are incorporated into this piece:
scent, sight, sound, and touch. So if you can, read these brief
couple of paragraphs over again, and see if you can find each
of those elements, used at least once. Note, too, that perhaps
the most powerful detail comes from the use of sound, in the
sense of *words* spoken aloud (that is, dialogue). I chose to
include the real words that were exclaimed, in great dismay,
by my now twenty-one-year-old nephew, who upon seeing the
baby immediately after the birth did fear that his brother had
indeed been born dead. Fortunately, though, after ten or fifteen
minutes, the midwives were able to get the infant breathing. Yet
those first terrifying moments I've never forgotten—including the vivid sensory details, which definitely help bring the
scene to life. But now, let's look at another example:

Summer Storm

I was petrified the whole hour-long drive home from the airport, that early June night when I returned from my solo trip to Chicago. An intense summer storm had suddenly swept up the coast from the South, and as I sped down the interstate, to a loud chorus of thunder and occasional streak of bright-white lightning crashing down in the distance, the rain was pounding down so hard I could barely see the cars whizzing by all around me.

Pressing on, though, squinting through the vast layers of fog that immersed me, desperately attempting to keep my wheels glued to the right lane, all I could do was take deep breaths, and count the minutes till I could pull off the highway at last. The only thing that kept me going was the thought of *him,* waiting for me—for all I wanted in the whole world was to see him again, and sink with relief into his warm, waiting, welcoming arms once more.

I was hoping, too, that he wasn't too tired, even though it would be late, surely past midnight, once I finally got there—and that he'd still be up, perhaps having even set the usual sensual scene for me. For of all the men I'd ever known, all the lovers I'd ever had, *he* was the one who really knew how to create an atmosphere—one that made me instantly feel like I was floating on a fine cloud of sensual delight, and made me yearn to open my heart, mind, body and soul to all the wonders that were possible between a man and a woman.

He lived not far from me, in an elegant, spacious renovated apartment on the ground floor of a stately eighteenth-century brick house, set up high on a hill, and back from the road, surrounded by a field on one side and a thick forest on the other. From the first time I'd been there, I'd always felt right at home, too. Wonderful, warm colors abounded, from the pictures on the walls to the comfortable overstuffed furniture to the thick carpets that graced the handsome wide-planked wooden floors. And no matter what time of day or night, that place always seemed to be bathed in a lovely, misty light, whether from the soft rays of sun at dawn or from the candlelight at night. Much to my delight, too, he seemed to revel in the warm glow of candlelight as much as I did.

In fact, every time we made love, he set a couple dozen candles, of all sizes, shapes, and scents, ablaze, all over his bedroom—on the dresser, the night table, the many window ledges that looked over a peaceful forest scene— creating a magical, mysterious, swell of warmth, that only seemed to help light our inner fires to new heights at the same time. The air then became infused with the magnificent array of scents, from deep, rich chocolate to spicy orange-cinnamon to sweet lavender, to summery rose, to island ocean mist, to Caribbean breezes. He liked incense, too, just as I did, and so the house was always filled, and warmed, too, by the strong, musky scent of sandalwood, or rich pine, or amber-rosewood, or some other ancient Japanese or Indian blend that had an exotic

name like Fire Goddess, or Magical Moon, or Jasmine
Sanctuary—which fairly intoxicated me, almost as much as
the wine that was always an essential ingredient of our
sensual ritual, too.

For as we prepared to make love, we always indulged in
some variety of fine, smooth, rich silky French, Spanish, or
Italian wine: richly flavored, with a deep red color to match,
that glinted like rubies in the delicate glasses that we
clinked together, before sipping down the delectable
substance, all the while breathing in the powerful aromas
that once arose in some fine vineyard now a continent away.
But now, those heady, fruity scents and tastes were here
only to serve us, and to enhance our desire for each
other—which grew stronger by the moment, until we could
hold back no more. Then, we would begin to feel the heat
shimmering between us, ever stronger, as we began to feel
the need to touch each other all over, until we were
completely lost in the bliss of each other's bodies and all
the exquisite pleasure we were capable of creating together.

It was *this* scene that played over and over again in my
mind, as I pressed through the driving rain that was still
coming down stunningly hard, hoping against hope that he
was still awake, and that my fantasies would indeed soon be
fulfilled. And finally, after an hour that seemed like an
eternity, I was almost there, turning off at the exit, and
heading the last few miles west toward my sleepy little
town—picking up speed as I approached that majestic old
house on the hill.

I smiled to myself with enormous relief, and anticipation, when I saw that the lights were still on in the kitchen and living room. The warm glow of candles, dozens of them, were indeed dancing, too, against every windowpane of that beloved back bedroom of his—which I'd come to think of as our own private haven, my oasis from *all* the storms that life brought my way. And I simply could not *wait* to get out of the car, and the cold rainy night, and inside, to the powerful warmth, magic, and love that awaited me in that heaven-on-earth kind of place.

As is often the case in my writing, this scene took a somewhat fictional twist, but began with a real memory of driving through a fierce rainstorm home from the airport, to be with the special man in my life.

As you can tell, many details are included here. I offer details of time and place from the start—letting the reader in on the fact that I was coming from the airport, and that it was early June. These details automatically invite the reader to visualize a certain setting and time of year, and naturally evoke different images and feelings than would be the case if I had described this as a winter storm, say, set in December or January.

This brief bit of writing is a good example of one that includes all five possible senses, too: Sight (the scene on the highway in the car, as well as inside his house), sound (the thunder and clinking of glasses); scent (candles and incense); taste (wine); and touch (the heat of each other's bodies). I believe that this rich combination of sensory detail makes for an emotionally evocative and enticing scene, that would be just a bit less vivid had any of those five senses been omitted. Now let's look at a third example:

Savannah Jewel

It was the year 1919, and divorce was almost unheard of, for any reason at all, especially in those parts of backcountry South Carolina. And his womanizing, and the weekly beatings—after awhile, somehow, she'd miraculously learned to take them. That kind of thing, wicked as it was, she thought she could bear living with. After all, her own mother had done the same for going on fifty years now. But finally—she knew, that *this* was it, the day after he'd forced her to have her fifth illegal abortion in four years' time.

Waking up at dawn to the relentless sound of the roosters crowing, in the oppressive, prison-like heat of their small isolated farm house on that dry, dusty late summer South Carolina day, the only thoughts that could fill her head were of the scorching afternoon of yesterday, in the doctor's smoky backroom, after the three-hour-long ride to Charleston. She could still feel his cold hands on her, old Dr. Richman, who reeked of tobacco, and had said not a word to her, and not looked, once, at her tear-strewn face, as he sliced her open, without anesthesia, to take the baby.

And it was there on that table, her mouth dry as a sheet of crumpled old sandpaper, gasping for breath, in that moment, the blood running down her legs, uncontrollably, the searing shock of it all even though she'd been through it before—that her heart had just about burst in two once and for all. And so it was this morning, so awash in shame, so deep in the pain that seemed to wrack her frail body from the inside out—that she knew she had no other choice.

So late that night, while Isaiah was still out drinking, weak and feverish as she was from the awful procedure, she bundled up her greatest life treasure—her small, still-asleep, still innocent six-year-old daughter, who smelled like the pale pink rose petals she'd been playing with that afternoon in the garden—Savannah Jewel. And she carried her, somehow, along with two huge old bulging suitcases to the rusted yellow car, with its rattling old engine that stood beside the aging barn, casting its ominous shadow across the long tobacco fields.

Laying her precious child on the back seat, kissing her softly on her warm forehead, she then covered her with the same thin white cotton blanket, embroidered with delicate yellow flowers along the edge that she'd taken comfort from as a young girl. She then stashed her suitcases, side by side, in the trunk, settled herself in the front seat, and turned the ignition, which, to her relief, fired up with a roar, without hesitation. With a look of fierce determination in her eyes, she then drove off into the darkness, the deep rural Southern landscape spread before her, without looking back—never to return, to that small town, that stifling house, or to his cruel demands, ever again.

This is the beginning of a fictional story I wrote a few years ago, based in part on the real-life experience of a friend's now-deceased great-aunt, who bravely chose to leave an abusive marriage in the days when divorce was rare indeed. I had a general sense of what had happened, in real life, but made up almost all of the sensory details that you find here to flesh out the story.

This story, too, includes all five senses. There is clearly much visual detail—including the descriptions of the car, the doctor's office, the child, and the blanket she was wrapped in, which add a much more realistic feeling to the story.

Sounds are present as well, including the "relentless . . . roosters crowing" and the ignition of the car firing up, "with a roar, without hesitation," as she prepares to drive away into the night. Scents include the tobacco smoke of the doctor and his office, which also brings up the associated sour taste of cigarette smoke. The taste of "sandpaper" in her dry mouth also is mentioned.

Several details of touch are also mentioned, including the doctor's cold hands as he performed the horrific procedure—which contrasts with the softness of her daughter's warm forehead as she lays her in the car in preparation for her escape. All work together to make for a dramatic and evocative scene of rural Southern life in a time long gone by.

And now, here's one last example from a story I wrote that starts with *sound* as an important element:

Footsteps

It was precisely three A.M., according to the stark, bright red numbers of the digital clock staring out at me coldly from the darkness as I awoke to a strange rustling noise—and then, the distinct and unmistakable sound of footsteps in the basement, right below my bedroom.

Shaken from my dream-state, I was immediately alert—and utterly petrified. I knew it had to be a burglar, who'd entered through the lower-level sliding glass door—and I was certain he had a gun, too, for there was no other explanation for the noises that were now crashing through my heart and were sure to reach my bedroom door in no time. And there was my five-year-old daughter, asleep beside me; we were alone, just the two of us in this huge house in the woods, just three months gone by now since her father had left us.

My heart was beating wildly, I could barely breathe, but I knew what I had to do. I reached for the phone, dialed 911, and whispered hoarsely into the phone. "Please help me! Someone's breaking into my house! I'm at 63 Harrington Road, the blue house, next to the pond!"

It was a terrifying ten minutes, which felt like an agonizing hour, till the policeman arrived. But when I heard his car pull up the long windy driveway, finally screeching to halt on the gravel right next to the house, I felt a slight wave of relief wash over me. The sweat had dampened my thin white cotton nightgown, though, and my heart was still pounding, fiercely, as I lay there, on the bed, utterly still, so afraid I would make a noise, any noise, for fear the intruder would know just where to find us. Now, though, safety, blessed protection, had arrived, the man in blue would take care of everything. He wouldn't let anyone hurt us. I *believed* this, wanted it to be true, and for his presence I was grateful beyond measure.

But ten minutes later? After a thorough search of the house, basement to attic, all he could say, in a dry and slightly sarcastic tone was, "I think you might have heard a chipmunk running around outside—or maybe you've got a mouse in the wallboards, I don't know, Ma'am—'cause there's absolutely nothing wrong that I can see—and no one else here—but *you*. You're absolutely and totally alone here."

And with that—he was gone. Leaving me alone, just as he'd said, with my daughter—and with my grief. And this fresh realization that he was right—that I really *was* alone, all alone in the world, no longer with a husband, a man of the house, to protect me from the worries of the world, and the wild fears of my own heart that had made me foolishly hear an ax-murderer in the sounds of a mouse scurrying about—brought on a fresh wave of the grief that I was constantly trying with all my might to fight off, as I made my way, hazily, through that first awful summer on my own.

Yet now, the floodgates had been unleashed—and for the rest of the night, I tried, without success, to get back to sleep. But I couldn't, because that dreaded storm of tears, once started, was just too hard to stop. Flooding through me wildly, they were simply beyond my control, forcing themselves out of me—tears of fear, fear of the unknown that was yet to come—tears of unending sorrow for the loss of my marriage—tears for my disappointed dreams— tears of deafening loneliness, they just kept coming— terrifying, tidal waves of tears. One after another, they rolled through me, before finally letting up, as I lay there, my pillow wet, my soul emptied once more, my body exhausted, just as the dawn broke, letting in streaks of pale purple and blue across the windowpanes.

   The sweet relief of sleep, then, mercifully, began to overtake me, and I could feel my eyes, heavy and damp and spent, finally closing. But just then, in that same moment, my daughter's sweet, soulful sapphire-blue eyes were opening—and peering expectantly, innocently, into mine. There she was, right next to me, her warm soft body offering comfort, smiling, laughing, ready to start the new day, never knowing what had transpired that night as she lay there dreaming. For I was the one whose dreams had been interrupted—my night dreams, as well as my daydreams, and my very life dreams—while she was only beginning to awaken to the awareness of what a dream even was.

This is based on a real-life moment I experienced a few months after my marriage ended. Various visual details are important here, from the "stark, bright red numbers of the digital clock" to the "sapphire-blue eyes" of my daughter. Yet rather than including all five senses, this piece emphasizes *sound* sensations above all—starting with the unwelcome and frightening sound that startled me awake, which I erroneously had thought was the footsteps of a burglar; the sound of the policeman's car in the driveway; and the sound of my sobs.

It's not always necessary to include all five senses, and there are times, such as in this scene, when deliberately emphasizing the details of one sense to a high degree can create the most powerful effect.

WRITING PRACTICE #9

Now it's time for *you* to do some more writing, incorporating as much sensory detail into your stories as you can. First, I'd like you to try this exercise: Write a short scene or story in which you focus on the effect of *sound* rather than sight (as you may be more used to doing) to see how emphasizing this sense to a greater degree can help your story become more exciting, lively, and realistic for your readers.

So if you can, start your story with a specific sound as a dramatic opening element. Then, incorporate other sounds, too, as you keep writing. Bring forth as many sound elements as possible, and consider how they can contribute to the emotional power of the scene you're describing.

The sound could be among the following:

A phone ringing

A baby crying

A truck screeching to a stop

Tell us the details...
Pay tribute
to all the everyday
& extraordinary
things...

Natalie Goldberg

Someone screaming

Someone's voice whispering in your ear

A siren going off

An alarm clock or bell

A school bell

A beeper

Ocean waves crashing on the beach

A gun being shot

A train whistle

A plane taking off

A noisy fight you are witnessing between your parents (or one that you're involved in yourself)

A radio blaring

A waterfall

A thunderstorm or any other kind of storm or heavy rain or wind

A tree falling over after it's been cut down

A chainsaw in the woods

A wasp or bee that's just landed on your shoulder or is buzzing too close to you for comfort

A dog barking loudly

A door slamming

A car crashing

A clock ticking too loudly

A musical instrument being played well, in a live concert—or practiced badly by a child

A cold, harsh, angry voice expressing disapproval of you

A loving, tender voice making you feel warm and safe and nurtured

WRITING PRACTICE #10

Now do some more writing, using sensory detail to draw the reader more fully into the world of your creation. You may want to go back to the same story you started in Key #3. Or, get started on a new story, using sensory detail very deliberately to paint an evocative scene with words. This time, see if you can write a story that includes all five sensory elements.

SUGGESTED TOPICS

↠ Find an old family photo and write a story about something that was happening in one of the lives of the family members at the time the photo was taken . . . and how that person's life changed in unexpected ways over the next ten years.

◆ Write a story about a time when you discovered a secret that you knew you shouldn't tell anyone, though you were burning to do so.

◆ Write a story about a day when your mother (or someone else very important to you) was furious with you.

◆ Write a story about the worst family holiday or vacation that you ever experienced . . . remembering to focus on specific *moments*, and describing them in great detail . . . infusing each scene with as much feeling as possible.

◆ Write a story about a time when you were trapped as a visitor in someone's house, or a school, or hospital, or anywhere else you really didn't want to be . . . for hours that felt like an eternity . . . and how relieved you felt when you finally got to leave.

◆ Write a story about a time when you had to deliver some bad news to someone, and how you went about doing it.

SUMMARY

Key #5: Focus on the Five Senses: Sight, Sound, Taste, Scent, and Touch

Remember, sensory detail is what adds feeling, depth, and power to writing, fiction or nonfiction. So from now on, become as aware as possible of how sensory details make for more powerful writing. Pay supreme attention to the details you use in your *own* writing—as well as to those that draw you in as you read the writing of others. Whenever you are reading—a newspaper or magazine article, poem, short story, novel, or anything else—notice just what details make the story feel compelling. What jumps out at you, helps you feel you know the characters, can imagine them clearly, and makes you care about what happens to them? What details will you remember later on, when you may be describing the story to someone else?

Become a master observer of how other writers use details judiciously—and hold it as your full intention to instill your own writing with as many details of sight, sound, scent, taste, and touch as you possibly can. For your true power as a writer can shine forth most clearly in the details that you generously and carefully offer to us, your potential readers—in each sentence, paragraph, and page of your writing.

Discover and Develop Your Own Unique Writing Voice

Key 6

Now that you've focused on bringing forth details of the five senses in your writing, it's time to consider the sound of the writing *itself*, as it flows through the reader's mind. For every piece of writing is infused with its own special sound, or *voice*—made up of the writer's choice of words; his or her unique way of creating and combining sentences; and the rhythm and distinct tone that is conveyed in each paragraph and page of writing.

We are ALL
capable of writing
in different styles...
So as you develop your
writing voice, always
be open, flexible
& experimental...

Caroline Joy Adams

And just as we all assume different tones of voice when we are speaking aloud, depending both on our mood and to whom we are talking—our husband or wife, child, business acquaintance, boss, coworker, mother, lover, neighbor, best friend, washer repairman, or bank teller—our writing voices, too, may vary considerably. Often, our writing voice depends both on our intended audience and the purpose our words may ultimately serve.

THE WRITING VOICES WE NATURALLY USE

We are all capable of writing in a great variety of styles. So consider the different tone, or "voice," you would use when composing each of these disparate pieces of writing:

A matter-of-fact list of things to do;

An apologetic letter to your child's teacher explaining why she's late for school;

A heartfelt letter to a dying relative;

An ardent, passionate love letter;

A persuasive business proposal;

An impersonal letter of complaint to a credit card company explaining that you've been wrongly overcharged for a purchase;

An editorial to the newspaper expressing concern about local or national events; or,

A work of fiction or nonfiction written from your deepest level of feeling or personal experience, which is perhaps *most* likely to bring forth your most readily identifiable, authentic writing voice.

The ability to write in different voices thus is available to everyone, just as it is for those of us who make a living from our writing. For while some professional writers stick to one genre and style most of the time, many other writers like the challenge of working in different forms according to their moods, needs, or interests at the time.

I know this is true for me—and I have written in just about every style imaginable, from the time I was first struck with a passion for writing at age five or six. And it's been with me ever since, inspiring me to write at one time or another all of the following: light-hearted nonfiction personal experience pieces; screenplays; a master's thesis in psychology; a serious textbook; inspirational poetry and books; and numerous short stories, my love of which has grown into this book on creative writing.

I have loved writing all of these works—and each one has a different tone and style. Yet disparate as my works are, I have a sense that my essential writer's voice shines through all of them—making each piece recognizable to those familiar with my writing.

EXPLORE MANY WRITING VOICES AND STYLES

Rather than feeling, then, that you must find and lock into one distinct, permanent style or writing voice—I highly recommend that you explore different writing styles, always with an attitude of flexibility and experimentation. For the more you are able to shift into new modes, styles, and ways of thinking—in life and in writing—the more joy, beauty, and pleasure you will be able to experience and create.

As you write more extensively, you'll become more clear about the kind of writing you're most drawn to creating. And you'll discover consistent elements that flow continuously through your writing, which you can begin to work on bringing forward to an even greater degree. For within each of us, there may well be one essential, unique writing voice that we find ourselves *most* comfortable with, which we can claim as our main style or voice, even though we can switch into subtly or dramatically different tones of voice at other times.

So let's examine a few examples now, as we consider just what makes for a unique, compelling, identifiable writing voice. First, let's take a look at the classic by Anne Frank: her *Diary of a Young Girl,* one of my own favorite books and a masterful example of the power of a writer's unique voice. This book is a diary written by a girl ages thirteen through fourteen, while she is in hiding with her family from the Germans during World War II. One of the world's most widely read books, it is highly personal and conversational in tone. The voice is deeply

The more you are able to
SHIFT into
New MODES,
styles, ways of thinking ...
in life, & in writing ... the more
joy, beauty & pleasure you'll
be able to experience & create ...

Caroline Joy Adams

intimate, giving you a potent glimpse of this young teenager's deepest thoughts and feelings about life. So take a look at this short excerpt from her diary entry of January 30, 1943:

from *Diary of a Young Girl*

I'm boiling with rage, and yet I mustn't show it. I'd like to stamp my feet, scream, give Mummy a good shaking, cry, and I don't know what else, because of the horrible words, mocking looks, and accusations which are leveled at me repeatedly every day, and find their mark, like shafts from a tightly strung bow, and which are just as hard to draw from my body. . . .

More than once, after a whole string of undeserved rebukes, I have flared up at Mummy: "I don't care what you say anyhow. Leave me alone. I'm a hopeless case anyway." Naturally, I was then told I was rude, and was virtually ignored for two days; and then, all at once, it was quite forgotten, and I was treated like everyone else again. It is impossible for me to be all sugar one day and spit venom the next. I'd rather choose the golden mean (which is not so golden), keep my thoughts to myself, and try for once to be just as disdainful to them as they are to me. Oh, if only I could!

This work, like most of the writing that appeals to me, has a feeling of great intimacy and immediacy, allowing me to feel that the writer is a personal friend, sharing her deepest, most pressing concerns, experiences, and feelings with me on a one-to-one basis. Here we find the distinct, honest, soul-searching voice of a young person who is truly trying to understand herself, those around her, and the challenging world she finds herself immersed in.

It's a powerful example of highly personal writing, told in the first person. Anne Frank writes, too, in short, clear, direct sentences, often sprinkling in dialogue of others, as well as including detailed description of what has happened to her in a given day's time.

Her true-life story, of course, had a tragic ending—yet her book lives on as a testament to the beauty and strength of the human spirit, even under the most adverse conditions. And while this was her one and only book, her writing voice—powerful, distinct, and personal as any writing can possibly be—will live on for the rest of human history, through those poignant pages that share so much of who she was and what she felt, thought, observed, hoped, dreamed, and yearned for in her fourteen short years on Earth.

Now let's look at another example, by a writer whose voice is also highly personal in tone. Written also from the first-person point of view, lending a feeling of immediacy and intimacy to the voice of the narrator, this is a fictional work by Millicent Jackson, a gifted young black woman who has been a participant in my regular weekly writing workshops. This scene is excerpted from her novel-in-progress. And right before the lines presented here, what has transpired in the story is that the character's mother has returned home, crashing her car into the garage as a result of once more being in a recklessly drunken state.

from *Broken*

I move in closer, to see if she's breathing. The rise and fall of her chest is minimal. Heavy footsteps filter in the silence. My father is back outside. He stands at a safe distance; peering into the car like a spectator of an accident he wants nothing to do with.

"Mom!" I pound on the dashboard. My voice breaks like static on a car radio going through the mountains.

But then, silence spills over once more. Until my father's raspy voice, weary, annoyed, and frustrated to no end at this replay of a scene he's witnessed way too many times before, says, "Jean, come out of the car. Can't you see that you're hurting people!"

My mother barely looks up, but raises her head just enough to be heard. "Leave me alone!" she growls.

A chill zigzags through my body. Leave her alone. Leave her *alone*. The words repeat themselves throughout my mind. I hate when she does this. Gets that little attitude of hers. The alcohol bestowing on her liberties she wouldn't ordinarily take, thrusting words to the surface of her conscious mind she normally never would say. Leave her alone? She should be glad that I *care*. A part of me wants to slap the living daylights out of her, slap her *so* hard that maybe something will sink into that head of hers so eventually the alcohol will wear off. Why does she have to

refuse to be normal, anyway? And why my uncle Marvin
would let her leave his house in this condition pisses me
off even more. But his drunk ass is just as bad as hers, if not
worse. Sometimes I *swear* she does this on purpose. It
seems like she likes the attention, needs it almost.

The character telling the story here is speaking in a voice full
of potent emotions—including anger and frustration about
what is happening in the moment, and perhaps about her life
in general.

The writer uses a style that is direct, descriptive, and employs
brief bits of dialogue to give us a clear sense of the characters
and their personalities. Her distinct use of language reflects
her cultural background, too, as does almost all powerful and
eloquent writing. For the voices we use in our writing simply
must feel like the true speaking voices of the characters we are
depicting, especially when we use dialogue to illustrate the
characters' spoken words or the thoughts running through
their minds. Millicent Jackson, I believe, has succeeded in
evoking for us a scene that feels authentic and compelling—
and this is in great part due to her use of a writing voice replete
with the richness of language that comes naturally to the characters she so vividly brings to life.

Now, let's take a brief look at two examples of writing from
the third-person point of view—that is, writing that describes
the experience of characters other than the narrator—which
results in a different kind of writing voice altogether. First,
we'll look at the opening paragraph of a book meant for young
people, called *Riding Freedom,* by Pam Munoz Ryan.

from *Riding Freedom*

After ten years at the orphanage, Charlotte wasn't like most girls her age. And who knew if it was growing up like a follow-along puppy in a pack of ruffian boys, or if it was her own spit and fire. But she never had a doll or a tea party. She couldn't sew a stitch and she didn't know a petticoat from a pea pod. Wild hairs sprang out of her brown braids, and her ribbons dangled to her waist, untied. Her frock was too big and hung like a sack on her small frame. Smudges of dirt always covered her, and instead of girl-like lace, for as long as anyone could remember, she wore a strip of leather rein tied around her wrist.

A great deal of fiction, including *Riding Freedom,* is written from a third-person perspective—meaning that the writer employs pronouns such as "he" and "she" throughout, and writes about his or her chosen characters from an *observer's* viewpoint. This allows several advantages. For one, it makes it possible to describe the main character's physical characteristics (as is the case in this opening to *Riding Freedom*), which is much harder to do when you are writing as if you *are* the main character. It can also allow for much more detailed description of other people in the story, and indeed of every scene that is presented—because it's not limited only to what can be seen directly through the character's eyes.

Yet does writing from this viewpoint affect the author's writing "voice"? Does it make for a more impersonal, detached style of writing? It can, and *sometimes* does, but it certainly doesn't have to. In fact, writing from a narrator's voice can at times offer us a fuller experience, sometimes by allowing us even to peek into the minds of more than one character. And in this way, we may feel just as drawn into the story and embroiled in the thick of the action as when a story is told from the highly personal storytelling voice of a first-person viewpoint.

Now let's take a look at one last example, by a master storyteller who almost always writes from a third-person perspective but manages still to convey a highly personal and compelling feeling—Danielle Steele, one of the most prolific American writers ever. Here are a few paragraphs from her bestseller, *The Promise.*

from *The Promise*

"Well, young lady? Did I keep my promise? Do you have the most spectacular view in town?" Peter Gregson sat on the terrace with Nancy, and they exchanged a glowing look. Her face was still heavily bandaged, but her eyes danced through the bandages and her hands were free now. They looked different, but they were lovely as she made a sweeping gesture around her. From where they sat, they could see the entire bay, with the Golden Gate Bridge at their left, Alcatraz to their right, Marin County directly across from them, and from the other side of the terrace, an equally spectacular city view towards the south and east. The wraparound terrace also gave her an equal share of sunrises and sunsets, and boundless pleasure as she sat there all day. The weather had been glorious since she'd gotten the apartment. Peter had found the place for her, as promised.

"You know, I'm getting horribly spoiled."

"You deserve to be. Which reminds me, I brought you something."

She clapped her hands like a little girl. He always brought her something. A silly thought, a pile of magazines, a stack of books, a funny hat, a beautiful scarf to drape over the bandages, wonderful clattery bracelets to celebrate her new hands. It was a constant flow of gifts, but today's was the largest of all. With a mysterious look of pleasure, he left his seat on the terrace and went inside. The box he brought back was fairly large and looked as though it might be quite heavy. When he dropped it on her lap, she found her guess had been correct.

Danielle Steele's writing voice here, as always, is clear, direct, warm, and descriptive, easily and effortlessly drawing us into the world of the characters she has created. This book centers around a dramatic love story and includes an intriguing cast of characters, all painted in highly realistic ways, whom we get to know intimately through the selective use of dialogue and the continual description of their inner feelings, as well as of the settings and circumstances in which they find themselves.

I always have a hard time putting a Danielle Steele novel down, and I leave the book feeling that the characters have become my lifelong, unforgettable friends. And to me, it's of no importance whether her work is considered "fine literature" or "mass market." A good story is simply a good story. I find it no wonder, then, that the writing voice of Danielle Steele is one of the most widely read on this planet, with her more than 650 million books in print.

Keep These in Mind as You Discover and Develop Your Own Writing Voice

Here are a few things I'd like you to keep in mind as you work on discovering and developing your *own* writing voice. First of all, read, read, read. Read everything you can—including one-paragraph editorials, essays, exposés, and thousand-page nonfiction books or novels when you have the time.

You don't have to read whole books, either. If you skim a few paragraphs of a great variety of books, even in the course of an hour's browse at a good bookstore, you'll get an instant education about the vast variety of writers' voices possible. And as you read, stop, pay attention, and *truly listen* to the tone of voice of the writer. Make it your goal to become more conscious than ever of just what aspects of the writer's voice attract you and draw you in.

So as you read, ask yourself what it is about the way a given writer uses language that you like or dislike. We all have our preferences. Do you like to be spoken to in a soft, gentle voice, that immerses you in its lyrical, rhythmic flow, washing over you like warm tropical ocean waves? Or do you prefer writing composed of crystal-clear, direct, short sentences, with stories relayed solely in a succinct, everyday, down-to-earth conversational style? And which kind of voice would you most like to emulate?

A USEFUL EXERCISE

As you ponder these questions, here's an exercise you might find helpful: Make a list of the ten books you've read over the course of your life that have had the *most* impact on you and emotional staying power. Then take a trip to a large bookstore or library and find as many of these volumes as you can. This can be quite fun and enlightening—and may make you feel you've gathered a great many of your long-lost friends together for a long overdue reunion.

If you can, make an afternoon or evening of this book-hunting expedition. Go through the stacks of both fiction and nonfiction, select your titles, and then make a handsome circle of your chosen favorite books on a table, desk, or clear floor space.

Next, take a peek inside each one, and get a grasp of the voice that jumps out at you. Will you find similarities of voice and style—or great differences? Will you find that most of the writing voices make use of the first-person point of view, recounting tales in a deeply personal, conversational, heartfelt sharing style? Or will you find that the writing voices you like best are those that are more impersonal and detached? Or perhaps those that delve into the mind of more than one character, and make use of the power of descriptive detail to the degree that a third-person point of view allows for more readily?

Take a few moments to contemplate those voices that have helped shape your own style, and perhaps have influenced the very way you think, react, and now process life. Think, too, about whether you have grown to like a different *kind* of voice, over time, than you once did. Is it possible you've come to like writing voices that are gentler, more soft-spoken and nurturing? Or are you now more attracted to powerful, direct writing voices than you once were?

Are you more attracted to female writing voices or to those of males? Or have you rarely, when picking up a book, even been aware of whether you are being spoken to in the voice of a male or female?

Thought-provoking questions, these are. You may not have ready answers, either. But that's fine. These questions are posed here to get you thinking—for the more conscious we are of the writing voices of others, and of what attracts us to them, the more we can discover and develop a writing voice of our own that feels right, natural, authentic, compelling, and true to who we are and how we want to come across to the world through our words.

And, if you do decide to undertake this book-hunting expedition along with your writing group (if you belong to one), I bet you'll find it will bring up many funny, happy, and insightful memories of long-lost—and long-loved—books and related topics that will truly enrich your writing discussions for some time to come. So try it if you can; I think you'll find it lots of fun, on your own, in a group—or even with one or two friends who share your passion for books and writing.

WRITING PRACTICE #11

Now it's time to do some more writing practice of your own, keeping these questions of writing voice utmost in mind. First, I'd like you to write a short story, from the first-person point of view, making use of dialogue as a key component. This will allow the realistic voices of your characters to come forward, and can be the best way to bring forth your own writing voice most clearly and easily, too.

As you write, think about whether you *want* to write in short, direct sentences—or whether a more flowing, lyrical, poetic-sounding style seems more natural to you. You may find it helps enormously to read your work aloud to yourself, too. And, if possible, tape-record it and then play it back and listen—*carefully.* This will give you a sense of the rhythm you have created with your words, and will often help you realize if your sentences are too short and choppy and may need to be drawn out, with key words added. Or you may become aware that your sentences are longer than you've realized, and can be improved by removing unnecessary words or phrases.

Whenever possible, too, include dialogue between at least two key characters. Perhaps open your story with a dramatic moment in time, when one person or the other says something important—something that may well be startling, infuriating, horrifying, amazing, or poignant.

Write from personal experience, as nonfiction if you like. Or, write as a fictional narrator, telling the story in his or her own voice, with the full intention of drawing your readers deeply into the scene emotionally, through your compelling use of descriptive language and carefully chosen, accurately portrayed dialogue.

POSSIBLE TOPICS

↬ Write about a time when you realized for sure that a key relationship was over . . . a romance, friendship, work relationship, or something else of significance . . . and show a dramatic ending scene.

↬ Write about a time when you were deeply ashamed or guilty about something you had done or were about to do . . . and portray a scene in which you admitted it to someone else.

↬ Write about a night when someone said something to you that made you feel immediately sad, outraged, or fearful . . . in person or on the phone.

↬ Write about a time when you were given a wonderful gift you'd always wanted . . . or a time when you were given a gift you hated, that felt totally inappropriate, that made you feel that the giver didn't understand or appreciate who you were or what was important to you at all.

↬ Write about a night or day in which a beloved person in your life died . . . and how you felt, who you were with, what was said . . . or when a new member of your family was born.

Writing

is an act of cherishing...
It is an act of
LOVE...

Julia Cameron

Writing Practice #12

Now, I'd like you to take that same story you just wrote—and write it from a different "voice," or point of view. If you can, make the switch from a first-person, "I" perspective, to the third-person perspective, telling the same story from an outside observer's point of view.

For instance, you may have written a story about the time a younger brother or sister was born, when you were eight years old, and how you felt both pride and joy and resentment and anger about this event, as it meant that you would lose some of your parents' devotion and attention. Now, though, I'd like you to write the story from an outside narrator's voice instead of your own. For instance, in version one, you may have written the story as follows:

> I was eight years old the night Henry was born, and my life changed—for the worse, of course—the minute he came home from the hospital. Suddenly all the attention went to this squalling little creature, and no one could have cared less about me anymore, or so it seemed. So even though I was *supposed* to love him, the awful truth was I also secretly *hated* him, right from the first.

In your second version of the story, written from an outside observer's third-person viewpoint, you might write the story as follows:

Johanna had been an only child till then, and she and her mother had done everything together—shopping, cooking, reading, visiting, cleaning, getting the house ready every night for Daddy's auspicious arrival, late at night, right before she went to bed. And because he worked so much, and was rarely ever home even on weekends or holidays (the law office seemed to *be* his life far more than she and Mummy were), the two of *them* had been an inseparable twosome, a team, her whole eight years of life. And she liked it that way. Had thought it would always be like that. But the instant her little brother arrived, with his ceaseless demands, his cries, his needs, his wants, his desires— Mummy somehow took it not only as her duty but her joy to fulfill them, every second of the night and day.

Johanna's whole world changed, then, in an instant, the day he came home from the hospital. And certainly not for the better, but far for the worse—as Mummy's affections shifted, leaving her feeling lost, lonely, abandoned, unimportant, and invisible. And that, she knew, was when the deep, unfettered, rising well of anger inside her, that had grown into an uncontainable rage by the time she was a teenager, *really* started.

Do try this exercise. Write a second version of *your* story, from an observer's viewpoint, and see just how your writing voice shifts and changes. You'll undoubtedly find this an eye-opening writing experience, as you use language in subtly different ways, and end up with a whole *new* voice telling the story. Being able to switch perspectives is one of the most important aspects of the art and craft of writing—and one of the very best ways to cultivate the power and potential of your writing voice.

SUMMARY

Key #6: Discover and Develop Your Own Unique Writing Voice

Every story, poem, article, or book that's ever been written conveys a specific voice—that of the writer, or of the characters portrayed, which are sometimes one and the same. We all have specific *kinds* of writing voices that we are drawn to as readers—just as we each have tendencies to write in a particular kind of voice: personal or detached, gentle and soft, or direct and dramatic. And a key part of the writer's journey is in the continual discovery of new writing voices of others, including those who entertain, amuse, enlighten, and provoke us through their choice of words.

But the real excitement comes from the process of self-discovery that occurs when we experiment with our own voice, and take on different tones at different stages in our life, or even in different pieces of writing we work on through a single day or night.

In writing, as in all other aspects of life, we should each be free to experiment and open to allowing new voices and ways of writing to flow through us at all times. For it's this state of continual creative receptivity to what comes that can allow the most potent and powerful words of all to flow through us—words that may even startle us, as characters we create speak through us in voices we may never have expected to hear, much less set down on paper.

So as you write, be forever open, flexible, and free. And let the words flow forth, like a mighty, rich, resonant, and unstoppable river. In this unrestricted way, you will find your unique, most eloquent and prolific writing voice. It *will* be one worth sharing with others, too. And that's what we'll focus on in the next and last chapter of this book. So please join me there in a moment, as we prepare to bring this very special writing journey we've embarked on together to a powerful close.

Gather the
Courage to Share
Your Work

Key 7

ESSENTIALLY, WHEN WE OFFER UP our written words for others to read, what we're doing is *sharing*. We're sharing what we know or perceive to be true—even who we are at our core. We're exposing the innermost layers of our psyches; revealing our deepest thoughts, feelings, ideas; and possibly even our most painful and traumatic life experiences.

Sharing ourselves in this intimate way can be scary, too, because it makes us vulnerable, opens us up to possible criticism from others, when they don't react in the way we're hoping to

We WRITE because
WE WANT
To CONNECT
with others, on deep levels...
to cross the bridges of culture,
of time, & of space, with
our words...

Caroline Joy Adams

what we have to say. Still, most of us press on, for we are motivated to write, at least at times, because of our powerful desire to be listened to, heard, acknowledged, and responded to.

For despite our fears, we write because we want to *communicate,* to open our world to the mind of another, so that we may feel understood and less alone. We write because we want to connect with others on deep levels; to cross the bridges of culture, of space, and time with our words; and to know that our words matter to others—and thus, that *we* matter—that we have made a difference to others. For creating deeper understanding and more powerful connections with other human beings is truly one of the most wonderful and exquisite purposes and results of our writing efforts.

How We Can Increase Our Chances of Getting a Positive Response

So what can we do to increase the chances of communicating effectively, so that we *will* receive positive responses to our writing? Once more, I think the best way to strengthen our writing, allowing us to gain as much confidence as possible about it, is to ask ourselves some key questions once we have a first draft. This way we'll see what we may want to rework—*before* showing our work to others. And this may save us a whole lot of grief later on.

So let's consider the following questions in detail, remembering first and foremost this rule: that stories are always about *people*—people who are involved in a conflict, which usually revolves around their longings, dreams, or desires, and their great attempts, successful or not, to satisfy those desires.

QUESTIONS TO ASK YOURSELF TO DETERMINE JUST WHAT MAY STRENGTHEN YOUR WRITING

1. *Is your story about a specific person or people and their quest to fulfill their desires?*

Are your characters compelling and believable? Are their conflicts interesting enough? What do *you* think is most compelling about the conflict you have presented? Do you think your readers will find it of interest, too? If not, what can you change to make it more interesting to a wider audience?

2. *What do your characters most want in life that they don't yet have?*

And are there some things that they have lost and are trying to regain? What exactly are they doing to get their needs and desires met? What drives them to take the actions that they take? Do we care what happens to them, are we rooting for them, do we want them to achieve their goals? What major dramas of their lives have taken place before the action of your story begins, which (perhaps through flashbacks) you may need to fill the reader in on?

3. Are there strong emotions present in your story?

Exactly what are the predominant emotions? Can you identify at least three specific emotions that you have called forth in your characters, such as fury, sadness, hope, anxiety, suspicion, jealousy, desire, or grief? What do you *want* your reader to feel while reading, and after they have finished the story? Do you believe that you have successfully evoked these emotions? If not, what can you do to portray them more strongly? (Refer back to Key #3, which speaks about the emotional journey you are taking your reader on.)

4. Have you started the story with a powerful beginning?

If not, what can you do to make it more powerful? And does the power and momentum continue with a logical, consistent flow to your story? Or would it help to rearrange any parts, to make it feel more consistent? Are there any parts that seem too repetitive, or parts that you may need to expand on to flesh the story out? (Refer back to Key #2, about powerful beginnings; then take a look at the *Who, What, Where, When, How,* and *Why* questions of Key #4, to clarify these questions further.)

5. Have you used enough sensory detail?

Are there places where adding a few key, telling details could strengthen your characters and your story? Or are there places where you've used details that aren't necessary, that may be best removed? (See Key #5 for a reminder about the importance and potential power of using sensory detail.)

6. *Have you included any dialogue, and if so, does it sound authentic?*

Does the dialogue add to the power and feeling of the story? Does it make us feel we understand and care about the characters to a greater degree? If not, change it, or take it out altogether. Some stories are better without much dialogue, as it's *only* helpful if it lends a sense of intimacy, immediacy, and authenticity to the story.

7. *Are you allowing your own writer's voice to come through clearly and using language in a powerful and dynamic way throughout?*

Are you using lively, high-energy words as often as possible? Are you using active verbs, keeping adjectives and adverbs to a minimum, in favor of rich descriptive details instead? Does the writing overall have a feeling of life and energy? (Again, see Key #5 for good examples of the use of sensory detail, and Key #6 for powerful examples of a writer's dynamic, vibrant, unique voice.)

8. *Is there a good sense of rhythm flowing throughout?*

Have you used different sentence lengths, some short, some medium, perhaps some long, to create an interesting texture, flow, and sense of balance to your work? Have you read it aloud, or into a tape recorder, to see where you might want to add or delete words?

9. *Do you like your story? How does it make you feel when you read it?*

Your instincts and intuition are often not far from the truth. If you are finding that you are bored or restless with your story, or parts of your story, your readers may well be, too. If that's the case, ask yourself what can you do to liven it up and make it an irresistible read, so that you will be proud of it and will want to read it time and again yourself.

I strongly believe that if you ask yourself these questions, you will gain key insights into what needs to be changed or strengthened in your stories. And remember, almost *all* writing needs to go through a process of change, rewriting, and revision once a first draft has been set down. Few of us come up with something that reads perfectly the first time, and almost any piece of published writing has gone through a very careful, editorial polish before the public ever sets eyes on it.

So don't expect perfection. Instead, be open to the process of reworking your writing—sometimes alone; sometimes with the help of a good friend who can see things more clearly than you can; sometimes with a professional editor—and sometimes, perhaps, with the help of a supportive writing group.

Writing Groups Can Help Give Feedback

As a leader of writing groups, I am, of course, highly in favor of them. I have seen many men and women come to a group for the first time, confessing a great lack of confidence, yet who have been enormously helped by the group's affirmation of their urge to write and the supportive comments others who share their passion for the written word have offered them. Some of us, I find, even do our best writing in the context of group energy, too.

Of course, finding the right group, one which is truly supportive and encouraging and where commentary is purely constructive and helpful, is very important. And I can only hope that if you seek out a group, you'll be fortunate enough to find one like this, which can truly nurture you and your writing instincts along. You may wish to try various groups in your area and see if you find one that really feels right, before settling into it.

But if you cannot find such a group that already meets? Try starting your own by putting up a notice in your local library or bookstore—and I bet before long you'll get a few fellow writers interested in joining you. (If you wish to receive guidelines for running a writer's group, please see my Web site, *www.ThePowertoWrite.com*, and you'll be able to order a special booklet that shows you just how to get such a group going, and how to run it to achieve the best results for everyone.)

The *most* important thing, though, to remember, if you are participating in a writing group or considering starting one is this: When in school, or even in college, many of us felt criticized by both teachers and other students, and indeed this may have been a contributing factor to our having shied away from writing at all for years on end afterward. So a great many

Embrace your fear... but don't allow it to stop you...

Caroline Joy Adams

of us have deep-seated fears of sharing our work in a group setting, based on our very real earlier experiences that may have been far more harmful to us as writers than helpful. That being the case, I believe, strongly, that we should try to create as positive and nurturing an atmosphere as possible for each other when we choose to meet in writing groups. For the very purpose of such groups, more than anything, is to foster each others' creativity, and encourage each others' unique writing voices to come forth, have a place to be listened to and appreciated—maybe for the first time ever.

I believe, then, that it is of enormous importance to speak to each other in such settings only in very kind, considerate, appreciative ways; to offer positive suggestions for change, perhaps, but always in a very supportive and affirmative manner. I have been fortunate that virtually everyone who attends my groups follows this unspoken rule. We do offer each other excellent feedback, carefully choosing to focus only on what may truly be helpful and perceived as such by the other group members. So I know that this is possible, and that you can encourage *your* group to do the same. And if you can hold this goal as your one guiding light, you'll be off to an excellent start—and will be able to create and then sustain a wonderful, supportive group atmosphere that will stimulate everyone present to do their best work and to allow them to feel *safe* sharing their work and their words, in a way that may be an entirely new and deeply gratifying experience for them. And that's a great gift we can bestow upon each other.

And—it may be helpful to note that even those of us who

are published, experienced writers (and workshop leaders!) have our own hidden fears of sharing with a group. I know I do. At times, I feel afraid to share my work—even with my own students. When it's my turn to read, almost without exception, my heart begins to beat faster; my throat goes dry; my voice becomes shaky; and my mind races with thoughts that my writing isn't good enough and that my students will realize that I'm no better than them—or, perhaps, not even *as* good as them!

Still, despite my fears, I choose to press on and to share my work with others anyway. Because my own urge to write and to be heard and understood seems to overpower my deep-seated and ever-present fear of rejection. (And I'm certainly glad that's the case.) So, I implore you, my writerly friend, to live with *your* fear—embrace it, acknowledge it, let it be present—but don't let it stop you. As you share more and more, you'll find your fear will naturally diminish, bit by bit—and the rewards of sharing will begin to surpass the fear, perhaps before long at all.

So now, let's move on to our two final writing practices—which address the very topic of overcoming fear—bringing our writing journey together to a resounding conclusion.

Writing Practice #13

I'd like you to write about a time when you were possessed by fear, but somehow found a way to move *through* it and reach the other side. So start by writing about a specific, significant

WRITING...
a gift that comes to us,
a gift we give ourselves...
A GIFT
we give to others...

Louise DeSalvo

moment when you were most gripped by this fear. But then, also write about at least one time or moment later on, when you had overcome this fear, and were feeling very proud of yourself for having done so. Of course, if you prefer to write fiction, you may write this as a scene with a character of your choice from either the first- or third-person perspective. But in any case, make the fear strong, urgent, and *compelling*— and the feelings of relief from having overcome it just as real, too.

POSSIBLE TOPICS

↔ Write about a time when you almost had a terrible accident, but managed to escape unharmed . . . (or did have an accident, and how it effected you at the time, and later, when you recuperated from it, physically or emotionally).

↔ Write about a time when someone you loved (or hated) caused you deep physical or emotional harm . . . and a contrasting time, perhaps years later, when you realized with great happiness that it no longer had an emotional power over you, that you'd moved on to a place of forgiveness or release of this memory.

↔ Write about a time when you lost something or someone of enormous importance to you and the deep fears this brought up in you . . . and then a contrasting, later time when you had accepted this loss and moved on with your life, or found a way to create something new in your life that helped to make up for this loss.

WRITING PRACTICE #14

Now, write a story or scene about a time when you were afraid that you were incompetent (or your fictional character was), but then worked hard over time to attain a higher skill level. Then, write about a later time when you realized that you had indeed made huge progress, had conquered your fears of not being good enough, and that you *were* truly capable after all, much more than you had once imagined you could be. And who knows: the subject of *this* story could even be about your experiences of gathering the courage to share your writing, once you've realized that you do have something worthy of sharing . . . which I am certain that you do.

SUMMARY

Key #7: Gather the Courage to Share Your Work

Sharing your writing with others can be scary, risky, and feel like a huge challenge, that's true. But just imagine this for a moment. What if we were *all* too afraid to share ourselves through our words? What would life be like, then? What would the world be like, devoid of the written word, if we all held back out of fear?

There wouldn't be newspapers or magazines, those potent forums that exist for telling the truth about our day-to-day lives, from the personal to the global, that we so count on to inform us of what is happening around us. There wouldn't be the vast libraries that house millions of volumes, representing those souls who once made the valiant choice to overcome their fear of ridicule or rejection and persevered to the end, thus offering us the vast volumes of drama and literature, science, art, or psychology that we now treasure.

There wouldn't be the thousands upon thousands of novels or volumes of short stories, either, that give us so much pleasure in reading; works that have illumined our own sensibilities, perhaps shaped our very ways of thinking and being in the world; works that may have sparked in us visions of who we can become or have transported us to worlds we never would have dared dream of visiting otherwise. What a great gift that these countless writers have bestowed upon all of us—and you can be sure that every one of them had to overcome their own fears along the way.

Every piece of writing, published or unpublished, must be seen as the great *gift*—unique, precious, unrepeatable—that it is. It's a gift we give *ourselves,* first: the gift of self-expression, the gift of using our creativity, the gift of acknowledgment that our stories, our lives, our feelings, experiences, thoughts, and words do matter. And it's a gift we offer the world, second—the gift of allowing another human soul to know us—and therefore, to get to know themselves better, too.

So know that your words, too, are gifts. Don't hide

them away or keep them to yourself. Polish those gifts by working hard to infuse your writing with power and energy (whether it's your stories, poems, memoirs, or whatever other forms your writing may take) so that they're as soul stirring as can be. Ask yourself and answer the questions that can strengthen your words; force yourself to get rid of what's not working; and let go of the past and move on to the new when you feel called to do so.

But whenever you can—whenever you know that you have something important to say, that may change, illumine, or enhance even one other life—*make the brave choice to share it.* For your writing can make a huge difference in the lives of others: those close to you, or those who live a continent away, who you'll never meet in person. More than you may ever know.

So let your voice rise up and be heard—that it may be added to the magnificent chorus of humanity. Stand up and be heard, even if it causes you to shake with fear as you do so. Because fear *will* be present—but your *presence* is far more important than the fear that tries to stop you. So invite the world in, to listen—to *your* unstoppable, beautiful, wise, and powerful presence—through the timeless, eternal gift of your words.

Resource Guide

These days, there are so many wonderful books, magazines, writer's conferences, and other ways for writers to access information and inspiration that it is truly amazing. Virtually all the books included in the bibliography are ones I highly recommend. And, all you need to do is take a trip to your local chain or independent bookstore, or to an online bookstore like Amazon.com, and you will find many of these titles—as well as some newer ones. Just look in the section labeled Writing, or in some stores, in the Reference or Publishing category.

So all I would like to offer you here are some of the top Web sites and magazines that I myself enjoy and most recommend for other writers, and that I think you will find most helpful. You, too, will certainly find up-to-date information about writers' conferences, online or on-campus writing classes, and much more, on these excellent Web sites or in the back sections of these magazines.

Top 5 Writers' Web Sites

www.WritingClasses.com

This site is run by the Gotham Writers' Workshop in New York City and offers a full array of online writing classes in every genre imaginable, including: Fiction, Memoir, Novel Writing, Mystery Writing, Comedy Writing, Poetry, Romance Writing, Screenwriting, Children's Writing, Business Writing, and much more. I have nothing but praise for their fine online courses, and if you happen to live in the New York City area, you can also take on-campus classes, all led by expert and very helpful instructors.

www.WritersOnlineWorkshops.com

This site is an offshoot of *WritersDigest.com*, and offers a similar array of online courses to those mentioned in *Writing Classes.com*. Also highly recommended, with reasonable fees and excellent instructors in all specialty areas.

www.WritersDigest.com

An excellent resource for writers of all levels. Here you will find information about *Writer's Digest* magazine, the vast array of excellent books on the subject of writing published by Writer's Digest Books, as well as tips on getting published, and much more. And if you sign up for the Writer's Digest online newsletter, you will be sent continual writing prompt ideas, such as those in this book, to spice up and enliven your writing and help you keep in a highly creative mode.

www.WritersMarket.com

This site is the place to go when you are ready to consider publication. It allows you, once you join, to access a database of thousands of agents, editors, and publishers—for an extremely low fee.

www.ThePowertoWrite.com

This is my own Web site, which offers information about the Power to Write Short Story and Poetry Contests I sponsor each season in coordination with Barnes and Noble, as well as my own, related writing contests. Please take a look and consider entering one of our contests. Winning entries will be published on the site, and those who win each quarter will receive $25 worth of free merchandise from the site as well.

Top 5 Writing Magazines

Writer's Digest

I have always loved this monthly magazine, which I truly believe is useful to writers at all levels and who write in all genres. It is always chock full of both good, solid information as well as insights and inspiration for writers, offered by a wide variety of established writers. I always find at least one article in each issue that makes a positive impact on whatever I am writing in the moment—and I am sure that you will, too. This is the most widely read writing magazine, one that you are sure to be able to find in any bookstore, library, or newsstand.

The Writer

The Web site for this excellent magazine, another great one for writers of all levels, is *www.writermag.com*. For some reason, the magazine (which is published in Wisconsin) is not always in the bookstores, but it should be, as it is an excellent resource, always containing inspiring articles, market listings, and information on workshops and conferences. Highly recommended.

Poets & Writers

This is a wonderful bimonthly publication, often available in bookstores, which features interesting articles and inspiring examples in each issue of both recent poetry and fiction. As well, it offers excellent information about workshops, contests, awards, grants, and retreats for writers.

Creative Screenwriting

This one may only be of interest to you if you are considering screenwriting, but I think it's a great magazine for *all* writers to peruse once in a while—as screenwriting has much to offer us in terms of helping us think about what makes a good story, using interesting characters and dialogue, and much more. They have an informative Web site, too: *www.creativescreen writing.com*.

Publishers Weekly

This is the magazine you will want to read if you are interested in the world of publishing. It comes out every week, and you will get an in-depth look at what current publishing trends are, and, of course, you'll get a sense of what is selling by checking out the fiction and nonfiction bestsellers of the week. Often available in libraries, bookstores, and on the newsstand.

Sources

Page vi, calligraphy quotation: "We are all writers and readers . . ." by Roger Angell from the foreword to the paperback edition of *The Elements of Style* by William Strunk, Jr. and E.B. White (Needham Heights, MA: Allyn & Bacon, 2000).

Key One

Page 10, calligraphy quotation: "I want to write but more than that . . ." by Anne Frank from *Anne Frank: The Diary of a Young Girl* (New York: Bantam Doubleday Dell, 1993).

Key Two

Page 44, writing sample of a powerful opening by Marlo Morgan from *Mutant Message Down Under* (New York: Harper Collins Publishers, 1994).

Page 45, writing sample of a powerful opening by Gavin De Becker from *The Gift of Fear*, New York: Bantam Doubleday Dell, 1997).

Page 46, writing sample of a powerful opening by Michael Ventura from a magazine article, "Beauty Resurrected," published in the *Family Therapy Networker*, January/February 2001 issue.

KEY THREE

Page 77, calligraphy quotation: "Once you know what the story is . . ." by Stephen King from *On Writing: A Memoir of the Craft* (New York: Simon & Schuster, 2000).

KEY FOUR

Page 98, calligraphy quotation: "Go deep and try and tell the truth . . ." by Eric Maisel from *Deep Writing, Seven Principles That Bring Ideas to Life* (New York: Tarcher/Putnam, 1999).

KEY FIVE

Page 104, calligraphy quotation: "Description composed of sensory detail . . ." by Rebecca McClanahan from *Word Painting: A Guide to Writing More Descriptively* (Cincinnati: Writer's Digest Books, 1999).

Page 124, calligraphy quotation: "Tell us the details . . . Pay tribute . . ." by Natalie Goldberg from the introduction to *The Essential Writer's Notebook* (New York: Peter Pauper Press, 2001).

KEY SIX

Page 135, Anne Frank from *Anne Frank: The Diary of a Young Girl* (New York: Bantam Doubleday Dell, 1993).

Page 137, excerpt from a novel-in-progress, *Broken*, by Millicent Jackson.

Page 139, Pam Munoz Ryan, *Riding Freedom* (New York: Scholastic, Inc., 1998).

Page 140, Danielle Steel, *The Promise* (New York: Dell Publishing, 1989).

Page 147, calligraphy quotation: "Writing is an act of cherishing . . ." Julia Cameron, *The Writer's Life: Insights from the Right to Write* (New York: Tarcher/Putnam, 2001).

KEY SEVEN

Page 164, calligraphy quotation: "Writing . . . a gift that comes to us . . ." Louise DeSalvo, *Writing as a Way of Healing: How Telling Our Stories Transforms Our Lives*, (San Francisco: HarperSanFrancisco, 1999).

Bibliography

Adams, Kathleen. *Journal to the Self: Twenty-Two Paths to Personal Growth.* New York: Warner Books, 1990.

Albert, Susan Wittig, Ph.D. *Writing from Life: Telling Your Soul's Story.* New York: Tarcher/Putnam, 1996.

Barrington, Judith. *Writing the Memoir.* Portland, Oregon: The Eighth Mountain Press, 1997.

Berg, Elizabeth. *Escaping Into the Open: The Art of Writing True.* New York: HarperCollins, 1999.

Brady, John. *The Craft of Interviewing.* New York: Vintage Books, 1977.

Cameron, Julia. *The Right to Write.* New York: Tarcher/Putnam, 1998.

———. *The Writer's Life: Insights from the Right to Write.* New York: Tarcher/Putnam, 2001.

Campbell, W. John. *The Book of Great Books: A Guide to the 100 World Classics.* New York: MetroBooks, Wonderland Press, 1997.

Daniel, Lois. *How to Write Your Own Life Story.* Chicago: Chicago Review Press, 1997.

Darnton, John. *Writers on Writing: Collected Essays from the New York Times.* New York: Times Books, 2001.

Daugherty, Greg. *You Can Write for Magazines.* Cincinnati, Ohio: Writer's Digest Books, 1999.

DeSalvo, Louise. *Writing as a Way of Healing: How Telling Our Stories Transforms Our Lives.* San Francisco: HarperSanFrancisco, 1999.

Duncan, Lois. *How to Write and Sell Your Personal Experiences.* Cincinnati, Ohio: Writer's Digest Books, 1986.

Eppel, Naomi. *The Observation Deck: A Tool Kit for Writers.* San Francisco: Chronicle Books, 1998.

Fryxell, David. *How to Write Fast (While Writing Well).* Cincinnati, Ohio: Writer's Digest Books, 1992.

Goldberg, Natalie. *The Essential Writer's Notebook.* New York: Peter Pauper Press, 2001.

Gross, Gerald. *Editors on Editing: What Writers Need to Know About What Editors Do.* New York: Grove Press, 1993.

Gunther, Irene, and Sharpe, Leslie T. *Editing Fact and Fiction: A Concise Guide to Book Editing.* Cambridge: Cambridge University Press, 1994.

Hood, Ann. *Creating Character Emotions.* Cincinnati, Ohio: Story Press, 1998.

hooks, bell. *Wounds of Passion: A Writing Life.* New York: Henry Holt, 1999.

Kelton, Nancy Davidoff. *Writing from Personal Experience.* Cincinnati, Ohio: Writer's Digest Books, 1997.

King, Stephen. *On Writing: A Memoir of the Craft.* New York: Simon & Schuster, 2000.

Klauser, Henriette Anne. *Put Your Heart on Paper: Staying Connected in a Loose Ends World.* New York: Bantam, 1995.

Lamott, Anne. *Bird by Bird: Some Instruction on Writing and Life.* New York: Anchor Books, 1994.

Leland, Christopher T. *The Art of Compelling Fiction: How to Write a Page-Turner.* Cincinnati, Ohio: Story Press, 1998.

Lukeman, Noah. *The First Five Pages: A Writer's Guide to Staying Out of the Rejection Pile.* New York: Simon & Schuster, 2000.

Maisel, Eric. *Deep Writing: Seven Principles That Bring Ideas to Life.* New York: Tarcher/Putnam, 1999.

Mandell, Judy. *Magazine Editors Talk to Writers.* New York: Wiley, 1996.

McClanahan, Rebecca. *Word Painting: A Guide to Writing More Descriptively.* Cincinnati, Ohio: Writer's Digest Books, 1999.

McCutcheon, Marc. *Building Believable Characters.* Cincinnati, Ohio: Writer's Digest Books, 1996. Reprint, New York: Tarcher/Putnam, 1999.

Meyer, Herbert, and Meyer, Jill M. *How to Write.* New York: Barnes and Noble Books, 1994.

National Book Award Authors. *The Writing Life: A Collection of Essays and Interviews.* New York: Random House, 1995.

Neubauer, Joan. *The Complete Idiot's Guide to Journaling.* Indianapolis, Indiana: Alpha Books, 2001.

Olsen, Tillie. *Silences.* New York: Delacorte Press, 1978.

Perry, Susan K. *Writing in Flow: Keys to Enhanced Creativity.* Cincinnati, Ohio: Writer's Digest Books, 1999.

Rabiner, Susan, and Fortunato, Alfred. *Thinking Like Your Editor: How to Write Serious Nonfiction and Get It Published.* New York: W. W. Norton & Company, 2002.

Reeves, Judy. *A Writer's Book of Days: A Spirited Companion and Lively Muse for the Writing Life.* Novato, California: New World Library, 1999.

Rozakis, Laurie E. *The Complete Idiot's Guide to Creative Writing.* New York: Alpha Books, 1997.

Rule, Rebecca, and Wheeler, Susan. *True Stories: Guides for Writing from Your Life.* Portsmouth, New Hampshire: Heinemann, 2000.

Spence, Linda. *Legacy: A Step-by-Step Guide to Writing Personal History.* Athens, Ohio: Swallow Press, 1997.

Stine, Jean Marie. *Writing Successful Self-Help and How-to Books.* New York: Wiley, 1997.

Strunk, William, Jr., and White, E. B. *The Elements of Style,* 4th ed. Needham Heights, Massachusetts: Allyn & Bacon, 2000.

Sullivan, K. D. *Go Ahead: Proof It.* New York: Barron's, 1996.

Tarshis, Barry. *How to Be Your Own Best Editor.* New York: Three Rivers Press, 1998.

Venolia, Jan. *Rewrite Right! How to Revise Your Way to Better Writing.* Berkeley, California: Ten Speed Press, 1987.

Waddell, Marie, Esch, Robert, and Walker, Roberta. *The Art of Styling Sentences: 20 Patterns for Success.* New York: Barron's, 1993.

Wolf, Robert. *Jump Start: How to Write from Everyday Life.* New York: Oxford University Press, 2001.